RUSLAN RUSSIAN 1

Fourth edition

КАРТА РОССИЙСКОЙ ФЕДЕРАЦИИ
MAP OF THE RUSSIAN FEDERATION

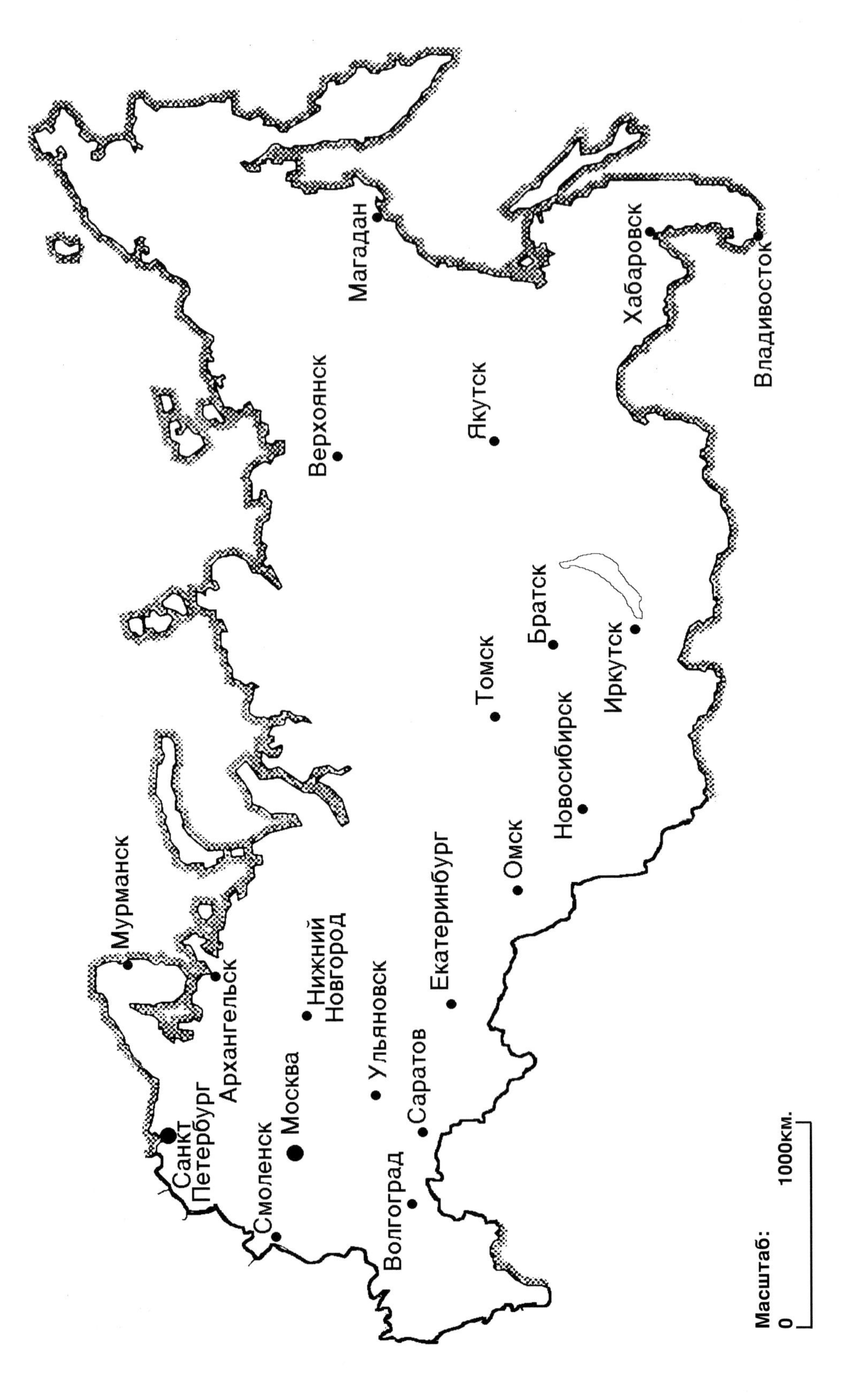

RUSLAN RUSSIAN 1

A communicative course for beginners in Russian
by John Langran and Natalya Veshnyeva.
Fourth edition.

Ruslan Limited
www.ruslan.co.uk

First published 1995
Second edition 1997
Third edition 2001, reprinted 2005
Fourth edition 2008

Ruslan 1 Textbook (fourth edition) ISBN 1-899785-65-5
Ruslan 1 Textbook and CD pack ISBN 1-899785-67-1

Errata
Any errors or amendments will be listed on the Ruslan website at:
www.ruslan.co.uk/errata.htm

Accompanying materials

Ruslan 1 Audio CD (4th edition)	ISBN 1-899785-66-3
Ruslan 1 Student Workbook	ISBN 1-899785-22-1
Ruslan 1 Reader	ISBN 1-899785-64-7
Ruslan 1 Teachers' notes	Free from www.ruslan.co.uk
Ruslan 1 CD-ROM	ISBN 1-899785-08-6

Ruslan Russian 2 and 3 continue the course to intermediate and advanced levels.

Ruslan Limited - www.ruslan.co.uk

INTRODUCTION

Ruslan Russian 1 is a beginners course in communicative Russian for adults and young people. The context is modern, with a clear and systematic approach. The course can be used by groups with a teacher or by individuals learning on their own. As well as the Ruslan 1 Textbook, there is a Student Workbook, a supplementary Reader, and a DTI prizewinning multimedia CDRom version. Here is a sample screen from the CDRom:

Try out the first lesson at www.ruslan.co.uk/demos.htm

The alphabet introduction describes the sound of each letter and gives examples in words. These are recorded on the audio CD and CDRom. There are also examples of Russian handwriting.

The ten lessons include:

- a list of contents for you to check your progress.
- a cartoon to help teachers introduce new vocabulary. These are also useful for practising questions and answers, and for revision.
- dialogues to introduce new vocabulary and structures, following the adventures of Ivan, Vadim, Lyudmila and her family and friends;
- a vocabulary with new words in the order in which they appear.
- background information in English.
- grammar explanations.
- exercises based on the new language.
- reading exercises with real or semi-real material.
- writing exercises to practise the handwritten script.
- listening exercises.
- speaking exercises, with role-play situations, and suggestions for pair work and language games.

At the end of the book you will find a key to the exercises, the texts of the listening exercises, a grammar summary, and a full Russian to English vocabulary for the Ruslan 1 course.

Acknowledgements
Thanks to all who have helped with this project, especially:
the Rossica Choir of St Petersburg, Olga Bean, Katie Costello, Ulla Frid, Paul B. Gallagher, Anna Garofalo-Kurman, Mikhail Kukushkin, Stef de Groot, David Harmer, Jelena Jefremova, Sergey Kozlov, Emma Lamm, Jonathan Madden, Tanya Nousinova and Brian Savin.

Photos are by John Langran, by people listed above, from Wikipedia, and from other public sources. Recordings are by people listed above.

Audio production is by Brian Savin and John Langran.

The authors
The authors are both experienced teachers of Russian to adults and young people.

Natalya Veshnyeva, who wrote most of the dialogues, was born and grew up in Moscow. She trained as teacher at Moscow Pedagogical Institute and has taught Russian at a wide range of schools and adult education centres in the UK and New Zealand.

John Langran, Director of Ruslan Limited, put the course together. John studied Russian at the University of Sussex, and taught in Birmingham, where he was head of Brasshouse Centre, Birmingham's language centre for adults. He has been Director of Studies for the Prime Minister's Enterprise Initiative in Russia, and author of the BBC Russian Phrasebook (1995 edition).

For teachers
Teachers Notes, tests, and other materials for teachers are available free of charge from the Ruslan website. The Teachers Notes give additional suggestions for classroom activities, hints on teaching difficult points, and additional photocopiable worksheets for each lesson.

Contact Ruslan Limited for a user name and password for the Ruslan teacher pages.

Ruslan Limited operates a scheme to help learners to find a local teacher. Details are on the website.

www.ruslan.co.uk

CONTENTS	СОДЕРЖАНИЕ

Dialogues marked (cd) 7 are recorded on the audio cd. The number is the cd track.
Where two numbers are given, the second is the same track with no sound effects.

Items marked (cd) www are available as free recordings from www.ruslan.co.uk/ruslan1.htm
www in the margin indicates that there is a note for learners at www.ruslan.co.uk/ruslan1.htm
Support for teachers, including free tests, is at www.ruslan.co.uk/tests/tests.htm

SOUNDS AND STRESS IN RUSSIAN

You don't need perfect pronunciation to be able to get by in Russian. It is likely to be obvious that you are a foreigner and people will be trying hard to understand you. But if you want to progress beyond a basic level it will be well worth spending time trying to pronounce the words as correctly as you can.

Russian pronunciation depends a lot on the stress. In words of more than one syllable there is one stressed vowel which is pronounced more strongly, or louder, than the others. The stress in Russian is unpredictable and has to be learnt.

In materials for learners, the stress is marked with an acute accent. For example the stress in the word for "wine" is on the last syllable - **вино́** - "veeno". But in the word for "problem" - **пробле́ма** - the "**о**" is unstressed and therefore reduced. It sounds more like the English "a" in "dad". Listen to these words in the Alphabet Introduction to check the difference.

In original Russian texts the stress is not marked. You have to learn it.

CYRIL AND METHODIUS

Cyril and Methodius
These were two Greek holy men, now Saints, who have been credited with the creation of the cyrillic alphabet.

In 863 AD they began a mission to convert the Slavic tribes to Christianity. In the process they translated the Scriptures into Old Church Slavonic, and created a Slavic alphabet based on existing Greek characters. Where there were no characters in Greek that corresponded to the sounds of Old Church Slavonic, they invented new symbols. The alphabet that they produced was amended at the time of Peter the Great, and again by Lenin in the 1920s.

In the days of the USSR, the cyrillic alphabet was in use in all the Soviet Republics. Today, as well as in Russia, cyrillic is the official script in the Ukraine, Belarus, Bulgaria and Serbia.

Abbreviations used in this book:

acc.	Accusative	instr.	Instrumental	prep.	Prepositional
adj.	Adjective	m.	Masculine	и т.д.	etc.
dat.	Dative	n.	Neuter		
f.	Feminine	nom.	Nominative		
gen.	Genitive	perf.	Perfective		
imp.	Imperfective	pl.	Plural		

THE RUSSIAN ALPHABET

The Russian alphabet has 33 characters: 21 consonants, 10 vowels and 2 phonetic signs.

2 Six letters are more or less similar in Russian and English:

а е м т о к

Examples in words:

а́том те́ма ма́ма коме́та кака́о такт

Six letters are “false friends”. They look like English letters, but their sounds are different:

в н р с у х

Examples in words:

торт ка́сса анана́с хор со́ус самова́р

3 The remaining letters are unlike English letters:

б г д ё ж з и й л п
ф ц ч ш щ ы э ю я

Examples in words:

бана́н	маргари́н	ви́за	ра́дио	репортёр
журнали́ст	зе́бра	кино́	май	сала́т
суп	телефо́н	цеме́нт	чемпио́н	шокола́д
борщ	Крым	эффе́кт	юри́ст	а́рмия

The two phonetic symbols (the soft sign ь and the hard sign ъ) have no sound of their own:

карто́фель объе́кт

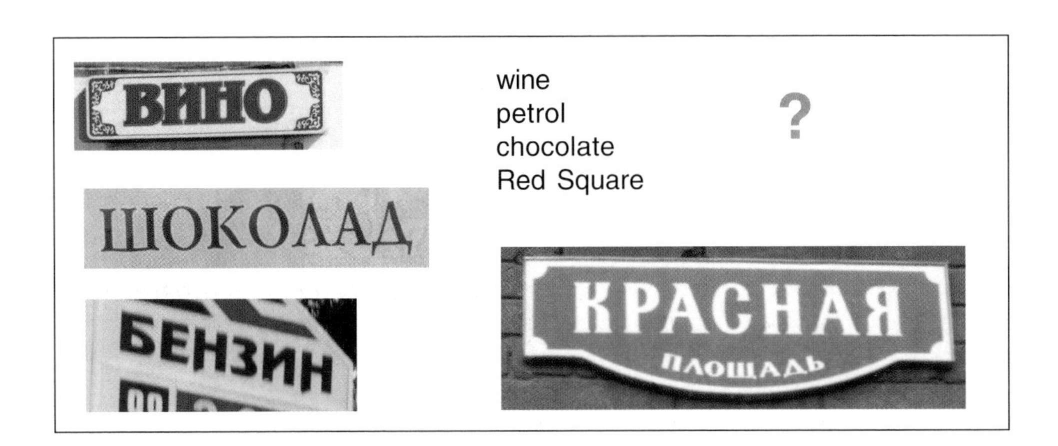

Letters and their sounds

А а stressed: "a" in "father", unstressed: "a" in "about".

Б б "b" in "bit". Sounds like "p" at the end of a word.

В в "v". Sounds like "f" at the end of a word.

Г г "g" in "gate". Sounds like "k" at the end of a word.

Д д "d". Sounds like "t" at the end of a word.

Е е stressed: "ye" in "yes", unstressed: "i" in "bit".

Ё ё "yo" - always stressed. Often hardened, as in "Горбачёв".

Ж ж like the "s" in "pleasure".

З з "z" in "zip". Sounds like "s" at the end of a word.

И и like "ee" in "eel".

Й й like the "y" in "boy".

К к "k" as in "kill".

Л л "l" as in "ball".

М м "m" as in "man".

Н н "n" as in "new".

О о stressed: "o" as in "for", unstressed: "a" in "about".

П п "p" as in "pan".

Р р a rolled "r".

С с "s" as in "sit".

Т т "t" as in "pat".

У у like the "oo" in "zoo".

Ф ф "f" as in "far".

Х х like the "ch" in the German "ach" or the Scottish "loch".

Ц ц like the "ts" in "tsar" or "hats".

Ч ч like the "ch" in "child".

Ш ш "sh" as in "sheep".

Щ щ long "sch" as in "borsch". Try to say "ee", keep your tongue in the same place, and say "sh" instead.

Ъ ъ "hard sign" - quite rare and has no sound of its own. Used to separate a hard consonant from a soft vowel.

Ы ы There is no equivalent in English. Start with "i" as in "bit", and then move your tongue lower and backwards.

Ь ь "soft sign". Has no sound of its own. It has the effect of softening the preceding sound.

Э э a hard "e", like the "e" in "when".

Ю ю a soft "u", like the first "u" in "usual".

Я я stressed: "ya" in "yak", unstressed: more like the "a" in "about".

Listen to the CD or use the CDRom for the correct sounds of the letters. There are some more detailed phonetic rules at: www.ruslan.co.uk/ruslan1.htm

www

THE ALPHABET - LETTERS IN USE

Letter	Example	Handwritten		Translation
А а	а́том	А а	атом	atom
Б б	бага́ж	Б б	багаж	luggage
В в	вино́	В в	вино	wine
Г г	грамм	Г г	грамм	gram
Д д	до́ктор	Д д	доктор	doctor
Е е	е́вро	Е е	евро	euro
Ё ё	ёлка	Ё ё	ёлка	New Year tree
Ж ж	журна́л	Ж ж	журнал	journal
З з	зоопа́рк	З з	зоопарк	zoo
И и	иде́я	И и	идея	idea
Й й	йо́гурт	Й й	йогурт	yoghurt
К к	кри́зис	К к	кризис	crisis
Л л	ла́мпа	Л л	лампа	lamp
М м	меню́	М м	меню	menu
Н н	ноль	Н н	ноль	zero
О о	о́пера	О о	опера	opera
П п	пробле́ма	П п	проблема	problem
Р р	рубль	Р р	рубль	rouble
С с	спорт	С с	спорт	sport

Т т	такси́	*Т т такси*	taxi
У у	у́лица	*У у улица*	street
Ф ф	футбо́л	*Ф ф футбол*	football
Х х	хокке́й	*Х х хоккей*	ice hockey
Ц ц	царь	*Ц ц царь*	tsar
Ч ч	чай	*Ч ч чай*	tea
Ш ш	шокола́д	*Ш ш шоколад*	chocolate
Щ щ	щи	*Щ щ щи*	cabbage soup
Ъ ъ	объе́кт	*ъ объект*	object
Ы ы	му́зыка	*ы музыка*	music
Ь ь	контро́ль	*ь контроль*	control
Э э	экспе́рт	*Э э эксперт*	expert
Ю ю	ю́мор	*Ю ю юмор*	humour
Я я	я́блоко	*Я я яблоко*	apple

The letter **ы** and the signs **ь** and **ъ** are never at the beginning of a word.

The stress marks are not used in authentic Russian texts.

In handwriting:
There are two versions of the letter "т" - *т/т*.

Some letters that are "tall" letters in English, for example "k", "l", are "short" in Russian: *к*, *л*.
They occupy just half the height of the line.

In *л*, *м*, *я* the "hook" at the start of the letter is clearly defined.

Some handwritten letters are quite different in upper and lower cases.

For more practice of the letters, use the Ruslan 1 Workbook.

LESSON 1	АЭРОПОРТ	УРОК 1

Ivan and Lyudmila meet on the plane and then arrive at Moscow Sheremetyevo airport from London.

You will meet a number of words associated with travel and arriving at the airport, and some basic questions and answers.

You will learn that:
- ❑ the Russians have no word for "the" or "a".
- ❑ the verb "to be" isn't used in the present tense.
- ❑ the intonation rises when you ask a question.

You will learn:
- ❑ some masculine and feminine words.
- ❑ the possessive pronouns "my" and "your" in masculine and feminine. forms - мой / моя́ and ваш / ва́ша.
- ❑ the pronouns он and она́, meaning "he" and "she" respectively, and both meaning "it".

There is some basic background information about Moscow.

By the end of the lesson you should be able:
- ❑ to read some notices at a Russian airport, and to understand several place names.
- ❑ to write some Russian letters, and to write your name.

> The **Ruslan 1 Workbook** contains 19 additional exercises for this lesson, including 3 listening exercises.
> The **Ruslan 1 Reader** has a text about Igor at Pulkovo Airport in Saint Petersburg, translation exercises, and a fun song for learners "Где ваш па́спорт?"
> The **Ruslan 1 CD-Rom** contains 23 additional exercises with sound. Lesson 1 of the CD-Rom is a free download at www.ruslan.co.uk/demos.htm

Is this the fast bus to the airport, or the slow one?

БУФЕТ
СУВЕНИРЫ
ПРИБЫТИЕ
ВЫХОДА НЕТ
ТАМОЖНЯ
НЕ КУРИТЬ
ТУАЛЕТ
М
Ж
ВЫДАЧА БАГАЖА
ПАСПОРТНЫЙ КОНТРОЛЬ
ВЫХОД
КОМПЬЮТЕР

Lyudmila and Ivan in the plane

6/11

Людми́ла: Здра́вствуйте!
Ива́н: Здра́вствуйте!
Людми́ла: Это Москва́?
Ива́н: Да, Москва́!
Людми́ла: Извини́те, вы тури́ст?
Ива́н: Нет, я бизнесме́н. А вы?
Людми́ла: Я тури́стка ... и ... журнали́стка.

Ivan at passport control

7/12

Official: Ваш па́спорт, пожа́луйста.
Ива́н: Вот, пожа́луйста.
Official: Вы тури́ст?
Ива́н: Нет, я не тури́ст. Я бизнесме́н.
Official: Вы Ива́н Козло́в?
Ива́н: Да, э́то я.
Official: Хорошо́. Вот ваш па́спорт.

Ivan and Lyudmila by the luggage reclaim

8/13

Ива́н: Это ваш чемода́н?
Людми́ла: Да, мой.
Ива́н: А где мой?
Людми́ла: Вы Козло́в?
Ива́н: Да, я Козло́в.
Людми́ла: Это ваш чемода́н?
Ива́н: Да, мой, спаси́бо.
Людми́ла: А су́мка ва́ша?
Ива́н: Да, спаси́бо.

Ivan going through customs

9/14

Official: Ваш биле́т.
Ива́н: Биле́т? Где он? А, вот он. Пожа́луйста.
Official: Где ваш па́спорт?
Ива́н: Где мой па́спорт? Вот он.
Official: А деклара́ция?
Ива́н: Вот она́. Пожа́луйста.
Official: Хорошо́. Вы тури́ст?
Ива́н: Нет, я не тури́ст. Я бизнесме́н.
Official: Где ваш бага́ж?
Ива́н: Вот мой бага́ж. Чемода́н и су́мка.
Official: А э́то что?
Ива́н: Это аспири́н.
Official: А э́то?
Ива́н: Это сувени́р.
Official: Хорошо́, вот ваш па́спорт и ваш биле́т.

Типи́чный англича́нин. Lyudmila notices a British visitor dropping some papers

10/15

Людми́ла:	Извини́те, это ва́ша ви́за?
Англича́нин:	Да, спаси́бо, это моя́ ви́за. А скажи́те, пожа́луйста, э́то Шереме́тьево?
Людми́ла:	Да, э́то Шереме́тьево.
Англича́нин:	Это Шереме́тьево-1 и́ли Шереме́тьево-2?
Людми́ла:	Это Шереме́тьево-2.

аэропо́рт	airport
Здра́вствуйте!	Hello!
э́то	this
Москва́	Moscow
да	yes
Извини́те!	Excuse (me)!
а	and / but
вы	you
тури́ст	male tourist
тури́стка	female tourist
бизнесме́н	businessman
журнали́стка	female journalist
нет	no
и	and
я	I
не	not
ваш / ва́ша	your (m. / f.)
па́спорт	passport
пожа́луйста	please / you are welcome
хорошо́	good
вот	here is
спаси́бо	thank you
чемода́н	suitcase
мой / моя́	my (m. / f.)
где	where
су́мка	bag
биле́т	ticket
он	he / it (m.)
деклара́ция	(customs) declaration
она́	she / it (f.)
бага́ж	luggage
что	what
аспири́н	aspirin
сувени́р	souvenir

типи́чный	typical
англича́нин	Englishman
ви́за	visa
Скажи́те!	Tell (me)!
Шереме́тьево	Sheremetyevo (airport)
оди́н	one
и́ли	or
два	two

типи́чный англича́нин

деклара́ция www
Travellers to Russia who are carrying more than a certain amount of foreign currency and valuables have to fill out a customs declaration form.

ви́за www
Foreign visitors must normally obtain a visa before entering the Russian Federation.

www

Москвá

Over 850 years old, Moscow is the capital of the Russian Federation, and with more than 10 million inhabitants (2005) it is the largest city in Europe. It is the "Port of Five Seas", which are linked to the city by rivers and canals. Moscow has four major airports, nine main stations, and a metro renowned for its efficiency, frequency, and amazing architecture.

www

English-speaking nationalities, male and female:

англичáнин	англичáнка	американец	американка
шотлáндец	шотлáндка	канáдец	канáдка
ирлáндец	ирлáндка	австралйец	австралййка
валлйец	валлййка	новозелáндец	новозелáндка

The Russians often use англичáнин / англичáнка to mean anyone from the British Isles!

ГРАММАТИКА

There is a glossary of grammatical terminology at www.ruslan.co.uk/ruslan1.htm

Articles and the verb "to be"

There are no articles ("a" or "the") in Russian, and the verb "to be" isn't used in the present tense ("I am", "you are").
You can therefore say a lot with just two or three words:

This is the airport.	Это аэропóрт.
I am a businessman.	Я бизнесмéн.
This is my luggage.	Это мой багáж.

The intonation of questions

In a question without a question word such as "what?" or "who?", the voice rises on the stressed syllable of the word you are asking about.

Это Москвá? - Is this **Moscow**?

Это ваш чемодáн? - Is this **your** suitcase?

The gender of nouns

Russian nouns can be masculine, feminine or neuter. You have only met the first two so far. Usually you can tell the gender by the last letter of the word.

Most masculine nouns end in a consonant or -й:

паспорт / багаж / турист / трамвай

Most feminine nouns end in -а , -я or -ия:

виза / Таня (the girl's name) / декларация

> In later lessons you will meet nouns with other endings.
> Nouns ending in -о or -е are almost always neuter.
> Nouns ending in -мя are neuter.
> Nouns ending in a soft sign -ь can be masculine or feminine.

Possessive pronouns

The possessive pronouns мой / моя - "my", and ваш / ваша - "your" agree with the noun that they refer to. Here they are either masculine or feminine.

Masculine	**Feminine**
мой паспорт	моя виза
мой багаж	моя сумка
ваш чемодан	ваша декларация

он / она

These mean "he" or "she" for people, and "it" when referring to things.

он is used to refer to a masculine noun:

Где ваш паспорт? - Вот он !

Где Иван? - Вот он !

она is used to refer to a feminine noun:

Где ваша виза? - Вот она!

Где Нина? - Вот она!

Здравствуйте! - Hello!

www

English speakers sometimes find this hard to pronounce.
If you have a standard English accent, try thinking of your donkey!
Say "Does your ass fit yer" fairly quickly and slurring the first "D".
The result is often very close to "Здравствуйте!".

The Russian equivalent of "Hi!" is: Привет!

Здравствуйте and Привет should only be used once a day, when you first meet. Привет should only be used informally, with people you know.

УПРАЖНЕНИЯ	EXERCISES	УРОК 1

1. Fill in the gaps with the correct word

а.	Где _______ журна́л?	ваш / ва́ша
б.	Это _______ ви́за.	мой / моя́
в.	Вот _______ биле́т.	ваш / ва́ша
г.	Где бага́ж? Вот _______.	он / она́
д.	Где моя́ су́мка? Вот _______ .	он / она́
е.	Где Людми́ла? Вот _______ .	он / она́
ж.	Где Бори́с? Вот _______ .	он / она́

2. Choose the correct response

а. Это ваш бага́ж?
б. Где ва́ша ви́за?
в. Вы тури́ст?
г. Вот ваш журна́л.
д. Это Ло́ндон?
е. Спаси́бо.
ж. Где ваш бага́ж?
з. Это нарко́тик?

Вот он.
Да, мой.
Нет, э́то аспири́н.
Пожа́луйста.
Вот она́.
Нет, я бизнесме́н.
Спаси́бо
Нет, э́то Москва́.

3. You have lost your passport. What might you say?

Это ваш па́спорт?
Где мой па́спорт?
Вот мой па́спорт.
Хорошо́.

Someone has found it. What might he / she say to you?

Это мой па́спорт.
Где ваш па́спорт?
Вот ваш па́спорт.
Спаси́бо.

You thank him / her:

Хорошо́.
Пожа́луйста.
Извини́те.
Спаси́бо.

And he / she might respond:

Хорошо́.
Пожа́луйста.
Извини́те.
Спаси́бо.

1. Notices at the airport. Work out which is which

www

ВЫДАЧА БАГАЖА	ТРАНЗИТ
№ РЕЙСА	КРАСНЫЙ КОРИДОР
НЕ КУРИТЬ	ПАСПОРТНЫЙ КОНТРОЛЬ
РЕГИСТРАЦИЯ	ТУАЛЕТ
СУВЕНИРЫ	ВЫХОД
ПАРФЮМЕРИЯ	ВЫХОДА НЕТ

Souvenirs - Transit - Check in - Luggage reclaim
Perfume shop - Red channel - No smoking - No exit
Toilet - Passport control - Exit - Flight number

2. What might interest a Russian customs officer?

билéт	пáспорт	вóдка
икóна	сувени́р	наркóтик
ви́ски	дóллар	журнáл "Экономи́ст"
декларáция	фотоаппарáт	газéта "Таймс"

3. Recognise the currencies!

Дóллар - Фýнт - Рубль - Евро
Япóнская иéна - Китáйский юáнь - Инди́йская рупи́я

4. Recognise the cars! Find three Russian cars!

Форд - Ренó - Мерседéс - Лáда - Фиáт - Ягуáр - Москви́ч
БМВ - Вóльво - Ситроéн - Вóлга - Кадиллáк - Тойóта

5. According to this list, which airport(s) would you use for the USA, for Western Europe, for Siberia?

www

www

Шеремéтьево-1:
Петербýрг, Мýрманск, Тáллинн, Ри́га
Шеремéтьево-2:
Лóндон, Нью-Йорк, Берли́н, Амстердáм
Внýково:
Волгогрáд, Ки́ев, Минск
Домодéдово:
Новосиби́рск, Хабáровск, Иркýтск, Лóндон, Пари́ж
Быкóво:
Ворóнеж, Владикавкáз, Сарáнск

Here is part of the passenger list from Ivan's flight to Moscow.

а. Work out who the three non-Russians are.
б. Add your own name in Russian handwriting, and the names of other people in your class.

1. Андреев Павел Борисович
2. Брансон Ричард
3. Иванов Борис Владимирович
4. Иванова Татьяна Николаевна
5. Козлов Иван Николаевич
6. Мальцева Юлия Павловна
7. Минский Вадим Степанович
8. Смит Мэри
9. Суханов Александр Львович
10. Тихонова Людмила Николаевна
11. Томас Джон Филип
12. Шишкин Михаил Андреевич
13. Щукина Зоя Борисовна

____

____

____

____

____

____

СЛУШАЙТЕ! LISTEN! УРОК 1

Listen to the dialogue on the audio CD

Людми́ла is going through customs:

1. Name the three items requested by the official for inspection.
2. What was the purpose of Lyudmila's trip?
3. Name the cities she has visited.
4. Has she any souvenirs?

You can use the text on page 129 to check your answers.

ГОВОРИТЕ! SPEAK!

1. Questions and answers about the cartoon on page 15

Это тури́ст? - Да.
Это сувени́р? - Нет, э́то телефо́н.
Где чемода́н? - Вот чемода́н.
Где па́спорт? - Вот он!
Где су́мка? - Вот она́!

2. Role-play (work in pairs)

You are at passport control. One person plays the border guard, the other plays a visitor. The visitor can decide whether to be a tourist (тури́ст), a business person (бизнесме́н) or any other profession that you know the word for.

Border guard
Ask to see passport.
Check status
(tourist / businessman etc).
Ask to see visa.
Return the passport and visa and say "thank you".

Visitor
Show your passport.
Say who you are.

Show your visa.
Respond.

Then change roles and start again.

3. Communication activity

This is for a group of people who are having their first Russian lesson. First choose your profession from the following:

журнали́ст - journalist
музыка́нт - musician
инжене́р - engineer

Then walk round the room, using Russian only, and try to find the people who have the same job as you, using words you have learned in this lesson.

- Извини́те, пожа́луйста, вы музыка́нт?
- Да, я музыка́нт.
- И я музыка́нт.
- Хорошо́!

- Извини́те, вы музыка́нт?
- Нет, я журнали́ст.

> Use just masculine forms. It would be unusual to use the feminine form журнали́стка in this situation. There is no feminine form of инжене́р or музыка́нт.

4. он / она́

Make a collection of objects or picture cards.
They should be either masculine or feminine. There are some pictures for you to use on the next page.

Ask each other questions and point when you give the answer.

> биле́т - во́дка - лимона́д - журна́л - компью́тер
> па́спорт - шокола́д - телефо́н - ла́мпа - су́мка

- Где журна́л?
- Вот он!
- Где во́дка?
- Вот она́!

5. или

Using the pictures opposite, ask and answer questions such as:
- Это биле́т и́ли па́спорт?
- Это па́спорт.
- Что э́то - шокола́д и́ли журна́л?
- Это журна́л.

www

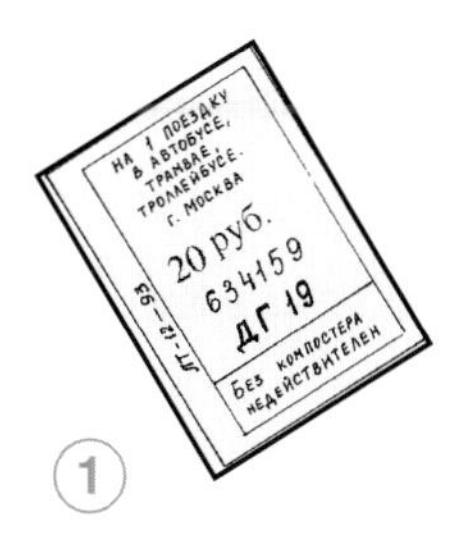

1

2

3

4

5

6

7

8

9

10

Ivan finds his way from Sheremetyevo airport to Arbat, a street in the centre of old Moscow.

In this lesson you will learn to ask some basic questions to find your way around a Russian town.

You will learn:
- ❑ how to say "I know" and "you know" - я зна́ю / вы зна́ете.
- ❑ how to use the prepositions в and на meaning "to".
- ❑ to recognise imperatives such as "Скажи́те!".
- ❑ да and нет, meaning nearly the same as "yes" and "no".
- ❑ the numbers 0 - 10.
- ❑ есть meaning "there is".
- ❑ the pronoun оно́, used for "it" when referring to neuter nouns.

There is information on Arbat Street in Moscow, a couplet from a song by Bulat Okudzhava, and there are photos of Moscow sights.

By the end of the lesson you should be able:
- ❑ to read an address in Russian.
- ❑ to recognise more place names.

The **Ruslan 1 Workbook** contains 16 additional exercises for this lesson, including 3 listening exercises.
In the **Ruslan 1 Reader**, Igor is looking for the Hermitage in Saint Petersburg, and there are photos of Saint Petersburg sights.
The **Ruslan 1 CDRom** contains 23 additional exercises with sound.

Many place names in Russia have been changed since the collapse of the USSR. On this map, "улица Вахта́нгова" is now "Большо́й Николопе́скевский переу́лок".

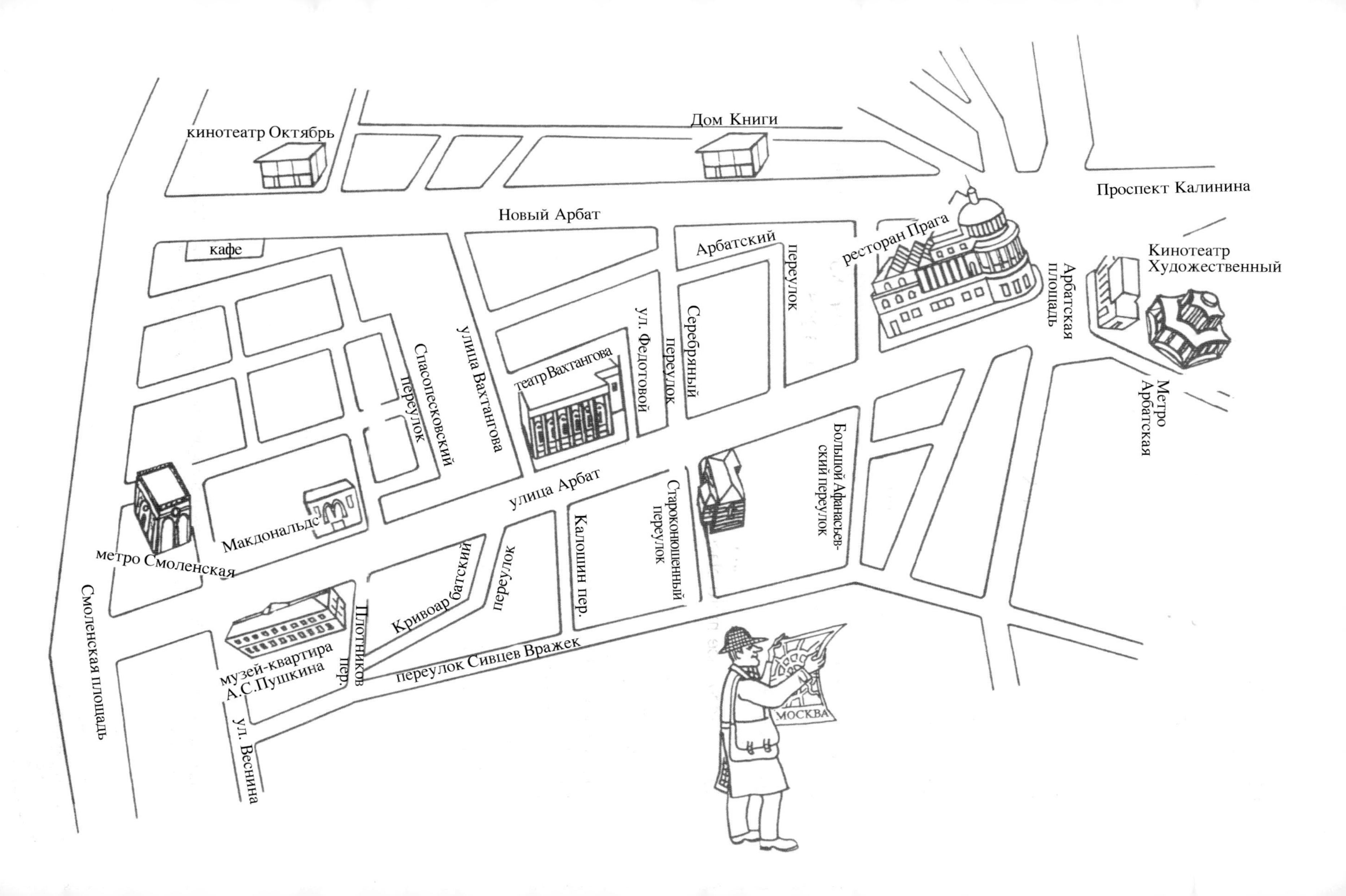
Проспект Калинина
Кинотеатр Художественный
Метро Арбатская
Арбатская площадь
ресторан Прага
Большой Афанасьев-ский переулок
Арбатский переулок
Дом Книги
Серебряный переулок
Староконюшенный переулок
ул. Федотовой
театр Вахтангова
Новый Арбат
улица Арбат
Калошин пер.
Кривоарбатский переулок
переулок Сивцев Вражек
улица Вахтангова
Спасопесковский переулок
Плотников пер.
кинотеатр Октябрь
Макдональдс
музей-квартира А.С.Пушкина
ул. Веснина
кафе
метро Смоленская
Смоленская площадь
МОСКВА

Ivan and Lyudmila at the airport

18/22

Ива́н: Извини́те, пожа́луйста.
Людми́ла: Да?
Ива́н: А, э́то вы? Тури́стка и журнали́стка?
Людми́ла: Да, э́то я.
Ива́н: Вы не зна́ете, где здесь метро́?
Людми́ла: Здесь нет метро́.
Ива́н: Здесь нет метро́?
Людми́ла: Да, нет метро́. Вот стоя́нка такси́, а там авто́бус.
Ива́н: Спаси́бо.

Ivan in the taxi

19/23

Ива́н: В центр, пожа́луйста.
Такси́ст: Куда́ в центр?
Ива́н: На Арба́т.
Такси́ст: Хорошо́.

They arrive

Такси́ст: Вот, пожа́луйста, Арба́т. Вот, нале́во, ста́нция метро́, а э́то у́лица Арба́т.
Ива́н: Спаси́бо.

Ivan in the street

20/24

Ива́н: Извини́те. Где здесь у́лица Вахта́нгова?
Прохо́жий: Я не зна́ю.

Ива́н: Где мой план? ... Ага́, вот он. Вот э́то Арба́т.
А где а́дрес? Улица Вахта́нгова, дом де́сять.
Хорошо́, вот э́то у́лица Вахта́нгова. Я здесь.
А что э́то? Теа́тр?

Ива́н: Скажи́те, пожа́луйста. Вы не зна́ете, где здесь теа́тр?
Прохо́жий: Теа́тр? Да. Теа́тр Вахта́нгова. Это бли́зко.
Иди́те пря́мо, и теа́тр напра́во.
Ива́н: Спаси́бо.

Типи́чный иностра́нец

21/25

Иностра́нец:	Извини́те, это Большо́й теа́тр?
Прохо́жая:	Большо́й теа́тр? Нет! Большо́й теа́тр не здесь.
Иностра́нец:	Я не понима́ю. А где Большо́й теа́тр? Это далеко́?
Прохо́жая:	Да. Это далеко́. Ста́нция метро́ "Театра́льная".
Иностра́нец:	Спаси́бо. А здесь есть метро́?
Прохо́жая:	Коне́чно. Вот оно́.

вы зна́ете	you know
здесь	here
метро́	underground
стоя́нка такси́	taxi rank
там	there
авто́бус	bus
в	to / at
центр	centre
куда́	where to
на	to / at
нале́во	to the left
ста́нция	station
у́лица	street
я не зна́ю	I don't know
план	plan / map
Ага!	Aha!
а́дрес	address
дом	house / block of flats
де́сять	ten
теа́тр	theatre
прохо́жий	male passer-by
прохо́жая	female passer-by
бли́зко	near
Иди́те!	Go!
пря́мо	straight ahead
напра́во	to the right
я не понима́ю	I don't understand
Большо́й теа́тр	the Bolshoy theatre
далеко́	far
есть	there is
коне́чно	of course (pronounced kanyéshna)
оно́	it

From the map on page 20:

кинотеа́тр	cinema
переу́лок	side street
пло́щадь (f.)	a square
рестора́н	restaurant

Звонова Зоя Петровна
РОССИЯ
115446 МОСКВА
ул. Вахтангова,
д.10, кв. 106
Тел.: 241 4345

Zoya Petrovna's visiting card - визи́тка. Note that the Russians write their address with the country first.

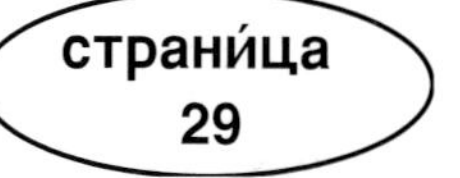

АРБАТ
Before the 1917 Revolution, Арбáт was a fashionable upper-class area of Moscow. After the Revolution it became a busy road full of small shops. During the period of "перестрóйка", Арбáт was the first street to be closed to traffic. Now it is used by artists selling their paintings on the pavement, and by sellers of souvenirs for tourists.

www

Ах Арбáт, мой Арбáт, ты моё призвáние.
Ты - и рáдость моя́, и моя́ бедá.
(Булáт Окуджáва)

Oh, Arbat, my Arbat, you are the meaning of my life.
You are both my joy and my trouble.
(Bulat Okudzhava)

www

Булáт Окуджáва
(1924-1997)

NUMBERS 0 - 10

www

0	ноль		
1	оди́н	6	шесть
2	два	7	семь
3	три	8	вóсемь
4	четы́ре	9	дéвять
5	пять	10	дéсять

ГРАММАТИКА

я знáю / вы знáете
Verbs in the present tense change their endings to agree with the person who is performing the action:

я знáю - I know
вы знáете - you know
я понимáю - I understand
вы понимáете - you understand

See page 52 for the full conjugation of **знать** - "to know".

The prepositions в and на

Both в and на can mean "to" in the sense of "to a place".

в центр	-	to the centre
на Арбáт	-	to Arbat

Practise saying "в центр" with no gap between the в and the ц.

As a general rule, в is used for enclosed spaces such as rooms, hotel, theatre, and на is used for open spaces, such as streets, fields, stations, etc. But there are many exceptions. Learn each example as you meet it.

напрáво / налéво and спрáва / слéва

напрáво / налéво are used when directing someone where to go:

Идúте напрáво!	Go right!
Идúте налéво!	Go left!

спрáва / слéва are used when saying where something is:

Теáтр слéва.	The theatre is on the left.
Ресторáн спрáва.	The restaurant is on the right.

Russians sometimes use напрáво / налéво in place of спрáва / слéва.

Скажúте!

Some verbs ending in -ите and all verbs ending in -йте are imperatives, to be used when giving commands or instructions.

Скажúте!	Tell (me)!	Читáйте!	Read!
Идúте!	Go!	Извинúте!	Excuse (me)!
		Слýшайте!	Listen!

да и нет

www

These do not mean exactly the same as "yes" and "no" in English. For example, the Russians often use "Да" to mean "Yes, there isn't", when in English we would say "No, there isn't".

- Здесь нет метрó?
- Да, здесь нет метрó.

есть - there is

The word есть is used on its own to mean "there is", or "is there?" in questions.

Здесь есть метрó? Is there a metro here?

Neuter nouns

Nouns ending in -о or -е are almost always neuter. The word for "it" for neuter nouns is онó.

- Где метрó?
- Вот онó!

1. Fill in the gaps in the sentences

а. Где ста́нция ________ ?
б. Где мой ______?
в. ________ пря́мо.
г. Это ва́ша _______?
д. Что вы не ________ ?
е. Скажи́те, ________, где теа́тр?
ж. Извини́те, я не ________
з. Теа́тр далеко́? Нет, ________
и. Это _______ план?

зна́ю
Иди́те
понима́ете
план
бли́зко
ваш
су́мка
пожа́луйста
метро́

2. Giving directions. Work out the answers

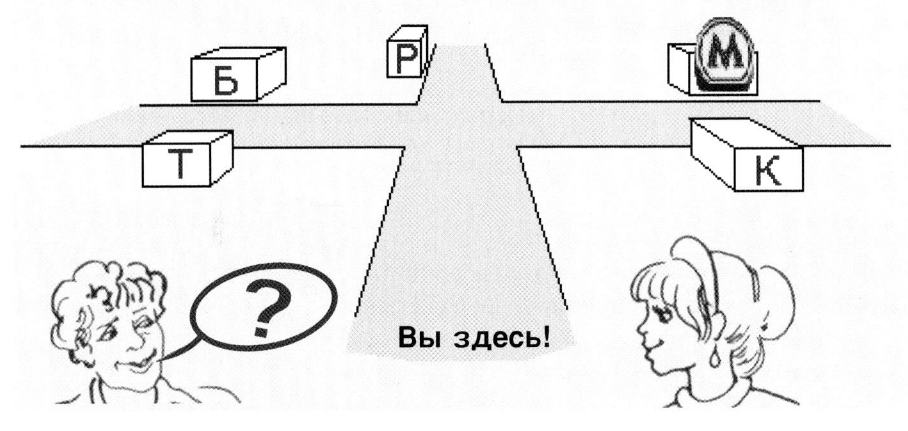

Скажи́те, пожа́луйста, где кинотеа́тр?
Скажи́те, пожа́луйста, где теа́тр?
Скажи́те, пожа́луйста, где буфе́т?
Скажи́те, пожа́луйста, где рестора́н?
Скажи́те, пожа́луйста, где метро́?

- Иди́те пря́мо и нале́во!
- Иди́те пря́мо и напра́во!
- Иди́те пря́мо!

3. Imperatives - which is which?

Иди́те! Скажи́те! Извини́те! Слу́шайте! Чита́йте!
Иди́те пря́мо! Иди́те напра́во! Иди́те нале́во! Пиши́те!

Go! Go left! Go right! Go straight on! Write!
Excuse (me)! Tell (me)! Listen! Read!

1. Can you read this list of cities?

www

Бирмингéм - Эдинбýрг - Бри́столь - Манчéстер
Лóндон - Кóвентри - Ливерпýль - Оксфорд

Try to say them with a Russian accent.
Write them out in Russian handwriting.

____

____

____

____

2. Here is the visiting card of a Western company's representative in Moscow:

СИМПСОН энд САН лимитед
Россия
119121, Москва
Арбатский переулок, дом 2
Николас Робертсон
тел.: (007) 495 241-12-12

What is the name of the company?
Can you find the street on the map on page 27?
What is the name of the representative?

Write out the address in Russian handwriting:

____

____

____

____

____

3. **Signs that you might see in the street. Which is which?**

МУЗЕЙ	МЕТРО
СТОЯНКА ТАКСИ	УЛИЦА
ТУРИЗМ	ИНТУРИСТ
КАССА	КИОСК
МЕДПУНКТ	ПРОСПЕКТ
МИЛИЦИЯ	РЕМОНТ
ТЕАТР	ЦЕНТР

Tourism - Theatre - Underground - Taxi rank - Kiosk
Under repair - Intourist - Museum - Ticket office
First Aid Point - Street - Centre - Avenue - Police

4. **Find the Russian towns in the maze**
(Чита́йте то́лько по-вертика́ли или по-горизонта́ли)

Ц Ц У Т О М С К М О С К В А
К Е Н Г З У Х Ъ Ф Ы В А П Р
О П Е Т Е Р Б У Р Г О Л Д Ж
Ф Е Я Ч С М М И Т Ь Б Ю Ё Ё
Р Р Л В Л А Д И В О С Т О К
П М О Л Д Н Ц У К Е Н П О П
В Ь П Р О С С М Т С Ы Е А П
Й Ц У И Р К У Т С К Ц Ц К Е
А С А Р А Н С К А П О М С К

Moscow, Petersburg,
Irkutsk, Murmansk,
Perm', Vladivostok,
Saransk, Omsk, Tomsk

Ивáн is trying to find the office he needs to go to tomorrow 26

1. Which underground station did he ask for?
2. Is it very far?
3. Which street is his firm in? Find it on the map on page 27.

ГОВОРИТЕ!

1. Talk about the map on page 27

а. Ask the way to different places, and give the answers.

б. Pretend you are walking along Арбáт, from метрó “Арбáтская” to метрó “Смолéнская”. Point out what you see.

Start: -
Вот Арбáтская плóщадь.
Спрáва рестoрáн “Прáга”.
Идúте прямо ..., etc.

2. Role-play (work in pairs)
You are in the street. One person plays the part of the tourist, the other plays the passer-by.

Tourist	**Passer-by**
Attract the person’s attention.	Respond.
Ask where the restaurant “Прáга” is.	Say it is close by.
Ask where it is.	Tell him / her to go straight on and then the restaurant is on the right.
You’re sorry, you don’t understand.	Repeat the directions.
Say thank you.	Respond.

Then change roles and do it again.

3. **Memory game in Russian**
Memorise the street plan on page 32. Then test your memory against other people in the group, asking the way to different places.
- Где теáтр?
- Пря́мо и налéво.
- Да.
- Где метрó? Пря́мо?
- Нет. Иди́те пря́мо и напрáво.

4. **Your own town**
Draw a map of a real or imaginary town, including some of these places:
университéт - банк - аэропóрт - зоопáрк - стадиóн (stadium)
поликли́ника (policlinic) - метрó - теáтр - кинотеáтр - ресторáн

Talk about your town with other people in the group.

5. **Он / онá / онó**
Repeat exercise 4 on page 24, but use some neuter nouns as well, for example: винó, такси́, метрó.
- Где винó?
- Вот онó!

6. **Вы знáете Лóндон?**
Use the list of towns on page 33. Ask each other questions to find out which towns people know.
- Вы знáете Лóндон?
- Да, я знáю Лóндон.

Use an Internet search in cyrillic if you need to check the spelling of place names etc. in Russian. There is help on this at www.ruslan.co.uk/ruslan1.htm

7. **Number practice**
Write the numbers 0 - 10 on the board in figures.
The teacher or a learner calls out the numbers.
Two learners stand by the board to see who can point to the numbers first, as they are called out.
Another learner can keep the score in Russian.

8. **Use the pictures on page 25 for more number practice**
- Нóмер два, что э́то?
- Это телефóн!
- Нóмер четы́ре, э́то пáспорт и́ли ви́за?
- Это пáспорт.

9. **Use postcards or photos of Russian towns to practise и́ли - "or"**
- Это Москвá и́ли Санкт-Петербýрг?
- Это Москвá!
- А э́то?
- Я не знáю!

МОСКВА

www

Большо́й теа́тр

Улица Арба́т

Коло́менское

Бе́лый дом

Моско́вское метро́

Лубя́нка

Магази́н ГУМ

Храм Васи́лия Блаже́нного

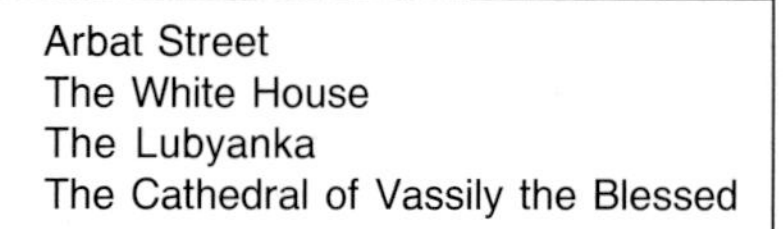

The Bolshoy Theatre	Arbat Street
Kolomenskoye	The White House
The Moscow Metro	The Lubyanka
GUM	The Cathedral of Vassily the Blessed

LESSON 3 СЕМЬЯ УРОК 3

Ivan arrives at Zoya Petrovna's flat and meets Lyudmila again.
Ivan needs somewhere to stay.

In this lesson you will learn:

- ❏ words to use when meeting people.
- ❏ the genitive singular of masculine and feminine nouns.
- ❏ the spelling rule for the use of the letters ы and и.
- ❏ some common uses of the genitive.
- ❏ that some common words of foreign origin never change their endings in Russian.
- ❏ how to use мóжно and нельзя́ with мне and вам to mean "I can", "you may not", etc.

There is information about the Russian name system.

By the end of the lesson:

- ❏ you should understand the Russian name system and recognise some common Russian names.
- ❏ you will recognise the words for different members of the family.

The **Ruslan 1 Workbook** contains 20 additional exercises for this lesson, including 3 listening exercises.
The **Ruslan 1 Reader** has a text about Anton and Vera, a poem about Saint Petersburg, and photos of Moscow and Saint Petersburg.
The **Ruslan 1 CD Rom** contains 27 additional exercises with sound.

Семья́ царя́ Никола́я II

28

At the Zvonovs' flat the doorbell rings

Зóя Петрóвна: Сейчáс... сейчáс.
Ивáн: Здрáвствуйте. Вы Зóя Петрóвна?
Зóя Петрóвна: Да. А вы кто?
Ивáн: Я Ивáн Козлóв.
Зóя Петрóвна: Ах, Ивáн... Вы прямо из аэропóрта? Как хорошó! Здрáвствуйте! Ивáн, э́то Людми́ла.
Людми́ла: Óчень прия́тно.
Ивáн: Что? Людми́ла? Э́то вы?!
Зóя Петрóвна: Как!? Лю́да? Вы знакóмы?
Людми́ла: Да нет! Я знáю тóлько, что Ивáн бизнесмéн.
Ивáн: А я знáю, что Людми́ла тури́стка и журнали́стка.
Зóя Петрóвна: Что? Журнали́стка?
Людми́ла: Зóя Петрóвна, а мóжно кóфе?
Зóя Петрóвна: Да-да, конéчно, я сейчáс...

29

Ivan and Lyudmila on their own

Ивáн: Так вас зовýт Людми́ла?!
Людми́ла: Да, меня́ зовýт Людми́ла. А вас зовýт Ивáн.
Ивáн: А скажи́те, Людми́ла, вы из Москвы́?
Людми́ла: Да, а вы?
Ивáн: Я не из Москвы́. Я из Сарáнска.
Людми́ла: Сарáнск? Где э́то? Далекó от Москвы́?
Ивáн: Не óчень далекó. Так вы знáете Вади́ма?!
Людми́ла: Да, óчень хорошó знáю.
Ивáн: Понимáю.

30

The coffee arrives

Зóя Петрóвна: Вот, пожáлуйста, кóфе.
Людми́ла: Спаси́бо.
Ивáн: А мне нельзя́ кóфе. У меня́ от кóфе аллерги́я. Мóжно мне чай? ... А э́то, Зóя Петрóвна, для вас.
Зóя Петрóвна: Для меня́? Что э́то?
Ивáн: Сувени́р из Лóндона.
Зóя Петрóвна: Спаси́бо, Ивáн. Что это? Кни́га? Очень хорошó!
Ивáн: Зóя Петрóвна, мóжно мне останови́ться у вас до среды́?
Зóя Петрóвна: Нет, Ивáн, извини́те, нельзя́. Понимáете, здесь сейчáс Лю́да и Вади́м, а у меня́ тóлько три кóмнаты.
Людми́ла: Знáете, Ивáн, гости́ница “Марс” не óчень далекó.

Zoya Petrovna sees some papers on the floor

31

Зо́я Петро́вна:	Ива́н, э́то ваш биле́т?
Ива́н:	Нет, не мой.
Людми́ла:	Это биле́т Вади́ма.
Зо́я Петро́вна:	А э́то?
Ива́н:	Это, ка́жется, биле́т Людми́лы.

сейча́с	now / just a minute
кто	who
из (+ gen.)	from
как	how
о́чень	very
прия́тно	pleasant
знако́мы	acquainted
то́лько	only
мо́жно	possible
ко́фе (m.)	coffee
так	so
вас	you (object)
меня́	me (object)
мне	for me
нельзя́	not allowed
у меня́	I have (See lesson 5)
от (+ gen.)	from
аллерги́я	allergy
чай	tea
для (+ gen.)	for
кни́га	book
у вас	at your home / you have
останови́ться	to stay; to stop
до (+ gen.)	until
среда́	Wednesday
но	but
вам	for you
ко́мната	room
гости́ница	hotel
ка́жется	it seems

семья́	**the family**
сестра́	sister
брат	brother
сын	son
дочь	daughter
муж	husband
жена́	wife
мать	mother
оте́ц	father
ро́дственник	male relative
ро́дственница	female relative
племя́нник	nephew
племя́нница	niece
де́душка	grandfather
ба́бушка	grandmother
внук	grandson
вну́чка	granddaughter
дя́дя	uncle
тётя	aunt

Вас зову́т ... - Your name is ... (They call you ...)
Меня́ зову́т ... - My name is (They call me ...)
To ask what someone's name is use Как? - "How?"
Как вас зову́т? - What is your name? (How are you called?)
Меня́ зову́т Иван - My name is Ivan.

"Меня́ зову́т ..." and "Вас зову́т ..." are only used with first names and patronymic names (see page 43). To ask someone's surname use:

Как ва́ша фами́лия?	What is your surname?
Моя́ фами́лия Шмит.	My surname is Smith.

The genitive case

The Russians have no word for "of". They use the genitive case instead:

Это билéт Вади́ма.	It is the ticket of Vadim (Vadim's ticket).
Это билéт Людми́лы.	It is the ticket of Lyudmila (Lyudmila's ticket).

Masculine and most neuter nouns have the genitive singular endings -а or -я. Ивáн becomes Ивáна, Андрéй becomes Андрéя.

Feminine nouns change -а to -ы or -и and change -я to -и.
Людми́ла becomes Людми́лы, Натáша becomes Натáши (see spelling rule), Тáня becomes Тáни.

> **Spelling rule**
> ы cannot follow: г, ж, к, х, ч, ш, or щ. It is replaced by и.
> This is why the genitive singular of Натáша is Натáши.

Personal pronouns are used in the genitive after certain prepositions.
я becomes меня́ and вы becomes вас :

Это для вас.	This is for you.

The genitive after prepositions

The genitive is used with a large number of prepositions, some of which we met in this chapter:

из	Ивáн из Сарáнска	Ivan is from Saransk
от	далекó от Москвы́	a long way from Moscow
до	до Лóндона далекó	It's a long way to London
	до среды́	until Wednesday
для	сувени́р для вас	a souvenir for you
у	у меня́ билéт	I have a ticket

The genitive to express possession

The verb "to have" is rarely used in everyday Russian. Instead use у with the genitive. More on this in lesson 5.

у меня́	-	I have	у Ивана	-	Ivan has
у вас	-	you have	у Нины	-	Nina has

The genitive with нет to mean that there is "none of" something:

Здесь нет гости́ницы.	There is no hotel here.
У меня́ нет вóдки.	I have no vodka.

The genitive with the numbers 2, 3, 4

два телефóна	-	two telephones	четы́ре чемодáна	-	four cases
три кóмнаты	-	three rooms			

оди́н has feminine and neuter forms and два has a feminine form

однá ви́за	-	one visa
однó метрó	-	one metro
две кóмнаты	-	two rooms

Animate accusative

The accusative endings of singular masculine animate nouns are the same as the genitive. For example:

Вы зна́ете Вади́ма? - Do you know Vadim?

This is not a point to be learned at this stage. See Ruslan 2, lesson 4 for a full explanation.

Foreign words

Many words of foreign origin never change their endings:

ко́фе, такси́, метро́, бюро́, меню́

Such words are neuter, apart from ко́фе - "coffee" - which is masculine.

www

Impersonal expressions: мо́жно and нельзя́

Use these with мне and вам and other words in the dative (lesson 9):

мне мо́жно - I may (for me it is possible / permitted).

вам нельзя́ - you may not (for you it is not possible).

ИНФОРМАЦИЯ

Russians have three names:

the first name - и́мя,

the patronymic name - о́тчество,

and the surname - фами́лия.

Это Влади́мир Влади́мирович Пу́тин и его́ жена́ - Людми́ла Алекса́ндровна Пу́тина.

The first name - и́мя - usually ends in a consonant, or in -ь or -й for a man, and in -а, -я, -ия or -ь for a woman.

The patronymic name - о́тчество - is formed from the father's first name, adding -ович or -евич for a man and -овна or -евна for a woman.

Влади́мир Влади́мирович Пу́тин - Vladimir, son of Vladimir, Putin.

Людми́ла Алекса́ндровна Пу́тина - Lyudmila, daughter of Alexander, Putina.

The surname - фами́лия - usually ends in -ов, -ёв, -ев, -ин, -о́й or -ский for a man, or in -ова, -ёва, -ева, -ина, -ая or -ская for a woman.

Андре́ев / Андре́ева Каре́нин / Каре́нина

Козло́в / Козло́ва Ма́йский / Ма́йская

Most surnames with other endings are non-Russian names and do not change: Громы́ко, Шеварна́дзе, Ко́рбут

In formal or work situations it is normal to use the first name and patronymic: Влади́мир Влади́мирович, Людми́ла Алекса́ндровна.

Informally the first name only is used, and this often becomes a diminutive. Sometimes there are several different diminutives for the same name.

Людми́ла can be called Лю́да, Лю́дочка, Ми́ла, Ми́лочка or Лю́ся.

Серге́й can be called Серёжа, Серёга or Серёженька.

1. True or false - according to the story?

а.	Ива́н Козло́в - бизнесме́н.	Да / Нет
б.	Ива́н из Москвы́.	Да / Нет
в.	Людми́ла из Сара́нска.	Да / Нет
г.	Зо́я Петро́вна из Ло́ндона.	Да / Нет
д.	Сара́нск о́чень бли́зко от Москвы́.	Да / Нет
е.	У Людми́лы от ко́фе аллерги́я.	Да / Нет
ж.	Сувени́р из Ло́ндона для Вади́ма.	Да / Нет

2. Далеко́ и́ли бли́зко? By Russian standards!

а.	Сара́нск далеко́ от Москвы́?	Да / Нет / Не о́чень
б.	Новосиби́рск далеко́ от Москвы́?	Да / Нет / Не о́чень
в.	Хаба́ровск далеко́ от Владивосто́ка?	Да / Нет / Не о́чень
г.	Минск далеко́ от Смоле́нска?	Да / Нет / Не о́чень
д.	Бирминге́м далеко́ от Ло́ндона?	Да / Нет / Не о́чень

Ask more questions of the same type about other towns you know.

3. Fill the gaps with the correct alternative

а.	_______ мне ко́фе?	Мо́жно / Очень
б.	Я вас не _________.	понима́ю / понима́ете
в.	Скажи́те, у _____ моя́ су́мка?	вам / вас
г.	Вы хорошо́ _______ Ло́ндон?	зна́ю / зна́ете
д.	У меня́ нет ______.	ви́за / ви́зы
е.	Это далеко́ от ______________.	гости́ница / гости́ницы
ж.	Я не зна́ю, как ______ зову́т.	вам / вас
з.	Биле́т_____ меня́?	для / у
	Нет, он для _______.	ма́ма / ма́мы

4. Арифме́тика

а. Два плюс два?
б. Три плюс четы́ре?
в. Де́сять ми́нус оди́н?
г. Пять ми́нус два?
д. Шесть ми́нус два, ми́нус четы́ре?

Make up more sums of your own and ask each other in pairs.
Make sure the answers are not higher than 10!

Дми́трий Анато́льевич Медве́дев
и Влади́мир Влади́мирович Пу́тин.

1. Fill in the gaps in Zoya Petrovna's family tree

Work out who fits where by checking the first names and patronymics.

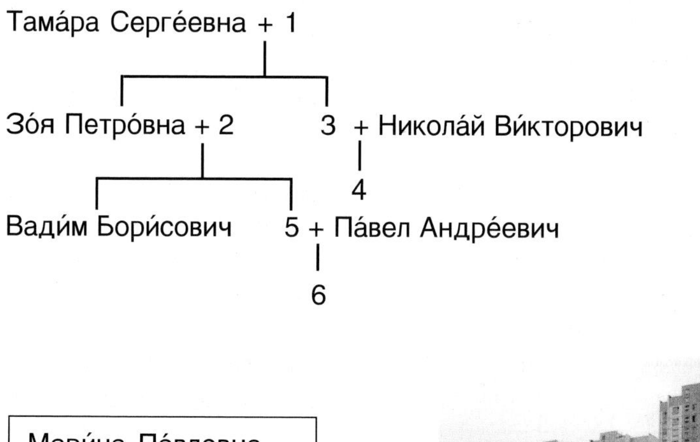

Мари́на Па́вловна
Гали́на Бори́совна
Ива́н Никола́евич
Ни́на Петро́вна
Бори́с Влади́мирович
Пётр Степа́нович

2. КЛУБ "ШАНС" - Match up the lonely hearts!

Меня зовут Елена. Мне 28 лет. Я из Волгограда. Люблю кино, театр, спорт. Я оптимистка. Мой телефон: 63-02-45.

Мне 35 лет. Я из Подольска, недалеко от Москвы. Люблю театр, балет и кино. Адрес: г. Подольск. Василий Нудин. Эл. почта: vnudin@mail.ru

Мне 30 лет. Я журналистка. Мои интересы: балет, опера, театр и классическая музыка. г. Москва, Почта: Ivanona267@rambler.ru Иванова Мария Алексеевна.

Меня зовут Егор. Я из Волково (недалеко от Волгограда). Я професссиональный спортсмен-футболист. Я люблю кино. Тел:(351) 84-16-75

Мне 28 лет	-	I am 28
эл. по́чта	-	email
я люблю́	-	I love

ПИШИТЕ! УРОК 3

Write out in Russian handwriting:

Two men's first names: ______________________

____

Two women's first names: ______________________

____

Two men's patronymic names: ______________________

____

Two women's patronymic names: ______________________

____

СЛУШАЙТЕ!

Людми́ла is talking to Зо́я Петро́вна about Ива́н 32

1. What relation is Ива́н to Зо́я Петро́вна?
2. Where does Зо́я Петро́вна come from originally?
3. What is her sister's name?
4. Do Ива́н and Вади́м know each other?

ГОВОРИТЕ!

1. **Как вас зову́т?**
   Ask each other's names. First use your real name. Then give yourself a Russian first name and do it again. Then give yourself a Russian patronymic and surname and do it again.
   - Как вас зову́т?
   - Меня зову́т Ива́н Петро́вич.
   - А как ва́ша фами́лия?
   - Моя́ фами́лия Ивано́в.

2. **Practice of the genitive**
   Make a set of cards with Russian names, one name per card. Pretend that they are people's tickets. One member of the group deals out the cards, and others have to say whose tickets they are.

   - Это биле́т Ната́ши!
   - Это биле́т Ива́на!

Бори́с - Ива́н - Степа́н - Оле́г - Вади́м - Макси́м - Влади́мир
Анна - Ната́ша - Ла́ра - Ни́на - Тама́ра - Людми́ла - Ири́на

3. Questions and answers on the cartoon page 39

Give people in the picture Russian names.
Speculate about who may be related to whom.
- Это Анна. И э́то Ири́на.
- Да.
- Это муж Анны?
- Нет. Это муж Ири́ны.

4. Го́род «Нет»

An exercise to practise the genitive after нет.
Ask each other questions about a town with no facilities at all!
- Где гости́ница?
- Здесь нет гости́ницы!
- Где рестора́н?
- Здесь нет рестора́на!

5. Role-play (for pair work)

You are helping a Russian visitor to the UK who is due to meet a small group of friends later today. They are:
Brian Jones, journalist, from Birmingham.
Peter Black, businessman, from Liverpool.
Mary Brown, student, from London.
Sharon Cook, journalist, from Manchester.

Prepare the Russian visitor for the meeting by explaining who the people are. Try to pronounce the names with a Russian accent. Add some more examples of your own.

6. Communication activity

Give everyone in the group a Russian name.
Then find a few objects that you know in Russian:

па́спорт - кассе́та - вино́ - во́дка лимона́д - биле́т - су́мка - сувени́р

One person goes out of the room, and the others decide which objects belong to whom. Then the person who went out comes back and has to guess who "owns" what, using the genitive ending:

- Это па́спорт Бори́са?
- Нет, э́то не мой па́спорт!

- Это вино́ Ната́ши?
- Да, э́то моё вино́!

Сувени́р из Москвы́

LESSON 4 ГДЕ ВЫ БЫЛИ? УРОК 4

Still at Zoya Petrovna's flat, Ivan meets Vadim.

In this lesson you will:

- ❑ learn to say where you have been and to talk about the past in a limited number of situations.
- ❑ meet the numbers 10 - 100.
- ❑ meet the months of the year.

The grammar includes:

- ❑ infinitives ending in -ать, -ить and -еть.
- ❑ the full present tense of знать - "to know".
- ❑ the basic rules of the past tense.
- ❑ the prepositional case, used with в and на meaning "at" a place.
- ❑ genitive singular endings of feminine nouns ending in -ия.
- ❑ ты - the familiar form of "you".

There is practice of writing a note in Russian in the past tense, and information about Russian National Holidays and about the New Year and Christmas in Russia.

The **Ruslan 1 Workbook** contains 19 additional exercises for this lesson, including 3 listening exercises.
In the **Ruslan 1 Reader**, there is a text about Anton and Vera's flat in Saint Petersburg, and a fun song for learners "Из аэропóрта в центр".
The **Ruslan 1 CD Rom** contains 29 additional exercises with sound.

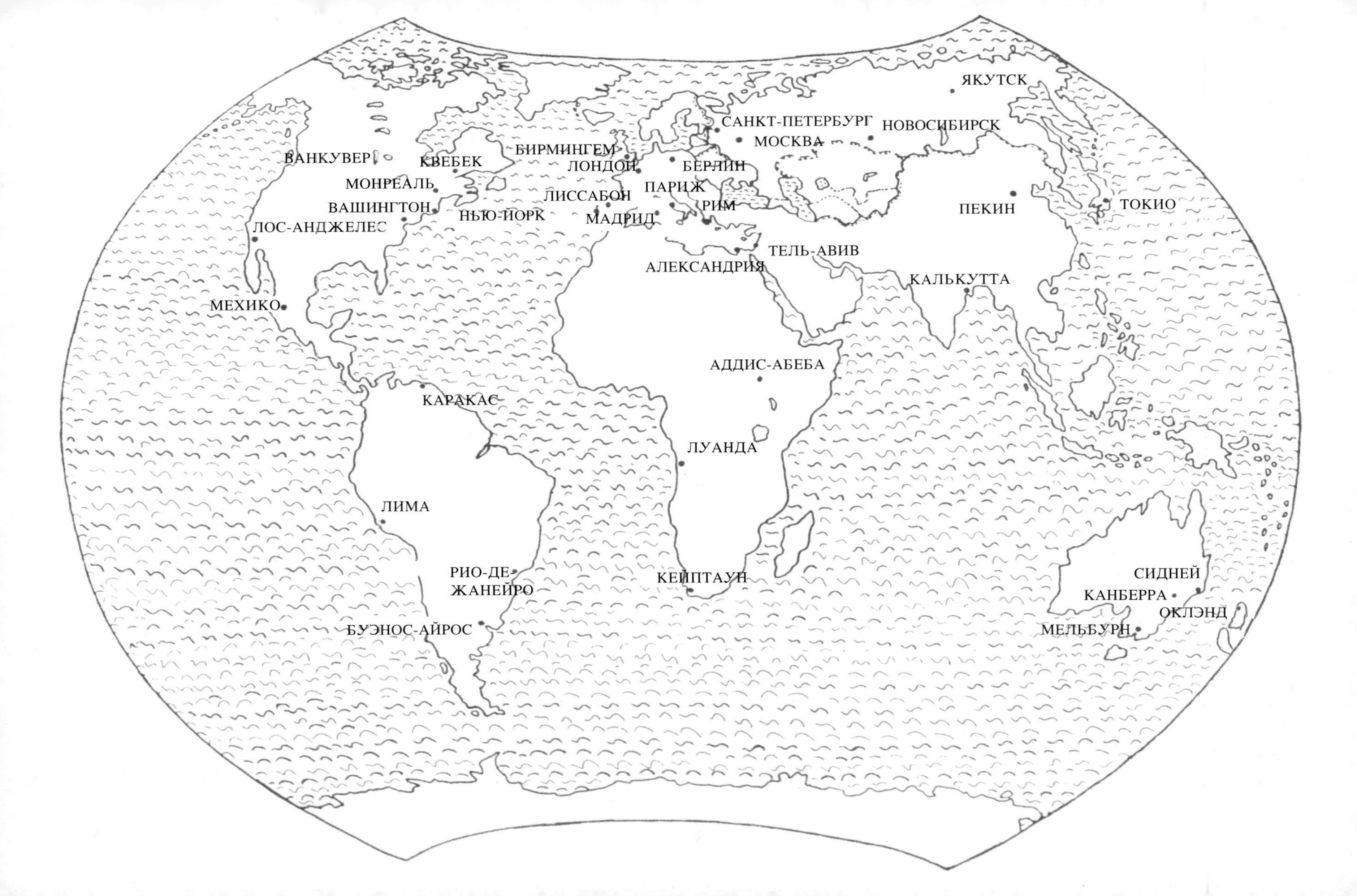
ЯКУТСК
САНКТ-ПЕТЕРБУРГ
НОВОСИБИРСК
МОСКВА
ВАНКУВЕР
КВЕБЕК
БИРМИНГЕМ
ЛОНДОН
БЕРЛИН
МОНРЕАЛЬ
ПАРИЖ
ЛИССАБОН
ВАШИНГТОН
НЬЮ-ЙОРК
МАДРИД
РИМ
ТОКИО
ПЕКИН
ЛОС-АНДЖЕЛЕС
ТЕЛЬ-АВИВ
АЛЕКСАНДРИЯ
КАЛЬКУТТА
МЕХИКО
АДДИС-АБЕБА
КАРАКАС
ЛУАНДА
ЛИМА
РИО-ДЕ-ЖАНЕЙРО
КЕЙПТАУН
СИДНЕЙ
КАНБЕРРА
ОКЛЭНД
БУЭНОС-АЙРОС
МЕЛЬБУРН

34

At the Zvonovs' flat

Зо́я Петро́вна: Так вы сего́дня пря́мо из Ло́ндона?
А что вы там де́лали? Рабо́тали?
Ива́н: Да, я рабо́тал. А что вы там де́лали, Людми́ла?
Людми́ла: Я уже́ говори́ла ...

35

The door bell rings

Зо́я Петро́вна: Я ду́маю, что э́то Вади́м. Я сейча́с...
Зо́я Петро́вна: Вади́м, проходи́ скоре́е, смотри́, кто у нас.
Вади́м: Людми́ла! Вот э́то сюрпри́з! А мы вас
сего́дня не жда́ли.
Зо́я Петро́вна: Мы жда́ли вчера́.
Людми́ла: Вот как?!
Вади́м: Ну, я о́чень рад вас ви́деть.
Людми́ла: Я то́же о́чень ра́да.

36

Зо́я Петро́вна: Вади́м, э́то Ива́н.
Вади́м: Ива́н?
Зо́я Петро́вна: Ива́н Козло́в... из Сара́нска.
Вади́м: Ах, ну да, коне́чно. Ива́н Козло́в из Сара́нска.
Коне́чно. Очень прия́тно! Сара́нск. Да, слы́шал.
Столи́ца Мордо́вии, да? Это далеко́?
Ива́н: Не о́чень далеко́. Три́дцать часо́в на по́езде.*
Людми́ла: Ива́н был в Ло́ндоне.
Вади́м: В Ло́ндоне? А что вы там де́лали?
Ива́н: Рабо́тал. У меня́ была́ командиро́вка в Ло́ндон.
Вади́м: Очень интере́сно! Бизнесме́н из Сара́нска рабо́тает
в Ло́ндоне?!

* Ivan didn't get this right. It is about 15 hours from Moscow to Saransk by train. Пятна́дцать часо́в на по́езде.

37

Зо́я Петро́вна: Вади́м, ты сего́дня обе́дал?

Вади́м: Да. Обе́дал. Так вы бизнесме́н?! Это о́чень интере́сно! А что вы де́лаете в Москве́?

Ива́н: У меня́ здесь то́же рабо́та.

Вади́м: Наве́рно, вы миллионе́р. У вас фи́рма в Москве́, и сего́дня вы пря́мо из Ло́ндона ... Очень интере́сно! А я Вади́м Бори́сович Зво́нов. Кинокри́тик. Вот, пожа́луйста, моя́ визи́тка. А вы, прости́те?...

Ива́н: Ива́н Никола́евич Козло́в.

Вади́м: Очень рад, Ива́н Никола́евич. Бизнесме́н, миллионе́р из Сара́нска. Прекра́сно! А где ещё вы бы́ли? В Вашингто́не? В Нью-Йорке? В То́кио?

Зо́я Петро́вна: Лю́да! Вади́м! Ива́н! Иди́те обе́дать!

Людми́ла: С удово́льствием, Зо́я Петро́вна.

Вади́м: Ива́н Никола́евич, проходи́те, пожа́луйста. А скажи́те, вы говори́те по-англи́йски...?

быть	to be
сего́дня	today (the "г" is pronounced "v")
вы де́лали (see grammar)	you were doing
де́лать	to do
рабо́тать	to work
уже́	already
говори́ть	to say / to speak
ду́мать	to think
Проходи́(те)!	Come through! (by foot)
скоре́е	more quickly
Смотри́(те)	Look!
сюрпри́з	surprise
мы	we
ждать	to wait
вчера́	yesterday
Вот как!	Oh really!
ну	well
рад (m.) / ра́да (f.)	glad
ви́деть	to see
то́же	also
слы́шать	to hear
слы́шал	I've heard
столи́ца	capital
три́дцать часо́в	thirty hours
на по́езде	by train
командиро́вка	business trip
интере́сно	interesting
ты	you (familiar)
обе́дать	to have lunch
рабо́та	work
наве́рно	probably
миллионе́р	millionaire
фи́рма	firm
кинокри́тик	film critic
визи́тка	visiting card
прости́те	I'm sorry
прекра́сно	wonderful
ещё	else / another
Иди́те!	Go! / Come! (by foot)
с удово́льствием	with pleasure
по-англи́йски	in English

Ру́сские бизнесме́ны в Бирминге́ме

ИНФОРМАЦИЯ УРОК 4

Moscow and the provinces. Saransk

To live in Moscow has long been a considerable privilege, and smaller cities in Russia are often regarded as somewhat provincial. Saransk is one of these. A city of some 350,000 people south east of Moscow, and capital of the republic of Mordovia, Saransk is a major producer of electric light bulbs.

Numbers 10 - 100

www

10	де́сять
11	оди́ннадцать
12	двена́дцать
13	трина́дцать
14	четы́рнадцать
15	пятна́дцать
16	шестна́дцать
17	семна́дцать
18	восемна́дцать
19	девятна́дцать
20	два́дцать
21	два́дцать оди́н
22 etc.	два́дцать два ...
30	три́дцать
31 etc.	три́дцать оди́н ...
40	со́рок
50	пятьдеся́т
60	шестьдеся́т
70	се́мьдесят
80	во́семьдесят
90	девяно́сто
100	сто

Months of the year

www

янва́рь
февра́ль
март
апре́ль
май
ию́нь
ию́ль
а́вгуст
сентя́брь
октя́брь
ноя́брь
дека́брь

The Russians use small letters for the months of the year.

Коло́менское в январе́

ГРАММАТИКА

Infinitives

A large number of infinitives in Russian end in -ать, -ить or -еть:

де́лать - to do   говори́ть - to speak   ви́деть - to see

The full present tense of знать - "to know"

я зна́ю	I know
ты зна́ешь	you know (familiar)
он зна́ет	he knows
она́ зна́ет	she knows
мы зна́ем	we know
вы зна́ете	you know (polite or plural)
они́ зна́ют	they know

Many, but not all, verbs with an infinitive in -ать conjugate in the same way.

The past tense

The past tense is formed by replacing the infinitive ending -ть with:

-л if the subject is masculine
-ла if feminine
-ло if neuter
-ли if plural

Ива́н не рабо́тал вчера́.	Ivan didn't work yesterday.
Людми́ла уже обе́дала.	Lyudmila has already had lunch.
Что вы там де́лали?	What were you doing there?

To say "was" or "were" use the past tense of the verb быть - "to be"

Masculine	- он / я / ты был	Neuter	- оно́ бы́ло
Feminine	- она́ / я / ты была́	Plural	- они́ / мы / вы бы́ли

Вади́м был в теа́тре.	Vadim was at the theatre.
Людми́ла была́ в Ло́ндоне.	Lyudmila has been to London.
Вы бы́ли в Вашингто́не?	Have you been to Washington?
Это бы́ло в Ки́еве.	It was in Kiev.

The prepositional case

This is used after в and на to say where someone or something is.
It answers the question где? - "where?".
Most nouns have the prepositional singular ending -е. This is added to most masculine nouns, and replaces the -а or -я for most feminine nouns.

Где ваш биле́т?	В су́мке.
Где Эрмита́ж?	В Петербу́рге.
Где рестора́н?	На Арба́те.

Masculine nouns in -ь replace -ь with -е

ию́нь в ию́не

Feminine nouns in -ь have the prepositional ending -и

Пермь в Перми́ (a town in Central Russia)
пло́щадь на пло́щади

Feminine nouns in -ия have the prepositional ending -ии

Росси́я в Росси́и

столи́ца Мордо́вии - the capital of Mordovia

Feminine nouns ending in -ия have the genitive ending -ии.

"ты" и "вы"

There are two words for "you" in Russian, the formal or plural вы and the informal ты. It is normal to use ты when talking to a child, and вы when talking to an adult, unless they are relatives or friends. Even with friends, it is advisable to wait for the Russian to invite you to change to ты. He or she will probably say:

Мо́жно на ты? - Can we use ты?

Смотри́! Look!

The -те ending on imperatives is left off when you are using the familiar ты form of address. Also "Здра́вствуйте!" has the familiar form "Здра́вствуй!".

УПРАЖНЕНИЯ УРОК 4

1. Find the correct answer according to the story

а. Что де́лал Ива́н в Ло́ндоне?
б. Людми́ла была́ в Ло́ндоне?
в. Ива́н из Москвы́?
г. Ива́н был в Ло́ндоне?
д. Вади́м обе́дал сегодня?

Нет, он из Сара́нска.
Да, он обе́дал.
Он рабо́тал.
Да, она́ была́ в Ло́ндоне.
Да, он был в Ло́ндоне.

2. Choose phrases to fill in the gaps

а. Большо́й теа́тр __________ Москвы́.
б. У Ива́на __________ три сувени́ра.
в. Сего́дня я обе́даю __________.
г. До Сара́нска 15 часо́в ___________.

в чемода́не
на по́езде
в це́нтре
в рестора́не

3. Choose verbs to fill in the gaps

а. Где вы __________ вчера́?
б. Вади́м не __________ в Ло́ндоне.
в. Зо́я Петро́вна то́же не __________ в Ло́ндоне.
г. Он уже́ __________ в Ло́ндоне и в То́кио.
д. Вчера́ мы __________ в рестора́не.

был
была́
бы́ли

е. Что вы _________ в Ло́ндоне?
ж. Вы __________ вчера́?
з. Он __________, что я __________ в Сара́нске.
и. Я __________ вас в рестора́не.

рабо́тали
был
знал
де́лали
ждал

4. Ива́н и Людми́ла. Put their conversation into the past tense

Ива́н: Что вы де́лаете в Ло́ндоне? ____________________________

Людми́ла: Я рабо́таю. ____________________________

Ива́н: А где в Ло́ндоне вы рабо́таете? ____________________________

Людми́ла: Я рабо́таю в це́нтре. ____________________________

Ива́н: А где вы живёте? ____________________________

Людми́ла: Я живу́ в гости́нице. ____________________________

5. Insert the correct form of the verb in the present tense

а.	Я не _________, где у́лица Че́хова.	знать
б.	Вы __________, что Ива́н миллионе́р?	ду́мать
в.	Где вы __________ сего́дня?	обе́дать
г.	Он ____________ в теа́тре.	рабо́тать
д.	Они не ___________ по-англи́йски.	понима́ть
е.	Ты ___________, где она́ ___________?	знать, рабо́тать
ж.	Мы ___________ в рестора́не.	обе́дать

ЧИТАЙТЕ!

Официа́льные пра́здники Росси́йской Федера́ции

1. Which months have the most official holidays?
2. Which Russian official holidays are the same as official holidays in your country?

www

НАЦИОНАЛЬНЫЕ ПРАЗДНИКИ

Но́вый год	1, 2 января́
Рождество́	7 января́
День защи́тника Оте́чества	23 февраля́
Междунаро́дный же́нский день	8 ма́рта
Пра́здник Весны́ и Труда́	1, 2 ма́я
День Побе́ды	9 ма́я
День Росси́и	12 ию́ня
День наро́дного еди́нства	4 ноября́

национа́льный	national
пра́здник	holiday
новый	new
год	year
Но́вый год	New Year
Рождество́	Christmas
день	day
защи́тник	protector
оте́чество	fatherland
междунаро́дный	international
же́нский	women's
весна́	spring
труд	labour
побе́да	victory
наро́дный	national

День Побе́ды

This list of Russian official public holidays was correct in June 2008. Any changes will be detailed at www.ruslan.co.uk/ruslan1.htm.

www

The Russians use the Orthodox calendar for religious festivals. As a result Christmas is on January 7th.

СЛУШАЙТЕ!

38

Людми́ла and Вади́м are having dinner

1. Is Vadim sure about Ivan's wealth?
2. Is Vadim a millionaire?
3. In which hotel does Lyudmila say she stayed in London?

ЧИТАЙТЕ И ПИШИТЕ!

Lyudmila received this note. Write her answer. Ask your teacher to check the result before you write up a final version.

39

Ресторан „Прага". Суббота.

Людмила!
Где Вы были? Я долго ждал сегодня в ресторане.
Может быть, Вы забыли?
Может быть, Вы работали?
Пожалуйста, позвоните.
Ваш Степан.

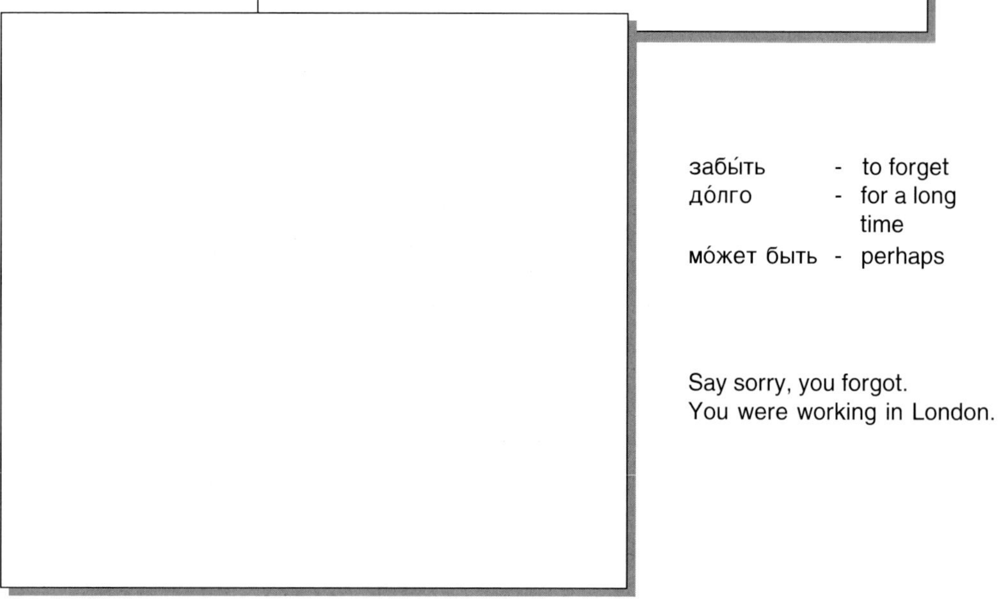

забы́ть - to forget
до́лго - for a long time
мо́жет быть - perhaps

Say sorry, you forgot.
You were working in London.

1. **Questions and answers about the map on page 49**
Talk about the map of the world. Which cities can you identify in Russian? Which places have you been to?
Ask each other "yes / no" type questions.

- Вы бы́ли в Мадри́де?
- Нет, я не́ был в Мадри́де.

The names of cities that do not end in -а, -я, -ь, -й, or in a consonant, are unlikely to change their endings.

2. **Pair work**
Which of these cities have you been to? Compare notes with different partners. Check the pronunciation of the city names with your teacher before you start:

Ло́ндон - Пари́ж - Берли́н - Санкт-Петербу́рг
Мадри́д - Ливерпу́ль - Москва́ - Чика́го
Бирминге́м - Амстерда́м - Нью-Йорк

- Вы бы́ли в Берли́не?
- Да, я был в Берли́не. А вы бы́ли в Амстерда́ме?
- Нет, я не была́ в Амстерда́ме.

3. **Communication game for a group**
An adaptation of "My grandmother went to market ...". Game for a group of not more than 6 people. The first person says where he / she was yesterday, using one building and one city. The second repeats this and then says where he / she was, and so on, around the circle.

For example:

Франк: Я был в рестора́не в Москве́.
Джу́ли: Франк был в рестора́не в Москве́, а я была́ в рестора́не в Ло́ндоне.
Пи́тер: Франк был в рестора́не в Москве́, Джу́ли была́ в рестора́не в Ло́ндоне, а я был в теа́тре в Ло́ндоне.
etc.

The last person has to remember everything, but others can help! Then work in pairs trying to remember as much as you can of who was where.

4. Кто миллионе́р?

Communication game to practise: “Я ду́маю, что...”
One person goes out of the room.
The others decide who is a millionaire - “Кто миллионе́р?“
The one who went out comes back, and has to guess:

- Я ду́маю, что Мэ́ри - миллионе́р
- Нет. Я не миллионе́р
- Я ду́маю, что ... и т.д.

5. Countries and languages

Ask people in the group whether they can speak various languages, and how well they can speak them.

- Вы говори́те по-францу́зски?
- Да.
- Вы хорошо́ говори́те по-францу́зски?
- Нет, не о́чень хорошо́.

Countries	**Languages**	
Великобрита́ния		
Англия	по-англи́йски	
Шотла́ндия		
Ирла́ндия		
Уэ́льс	по-валли́йски	
Аме́рика (США)		
Австра́лия		
Кана́да		
Новозела́ндия		
Фра́нция	по-францу́зски	Европа
Герма́ния	по-неме́цки	
Гре́ция	по-гре́чески	
Ита́лия	по-италья́нски	
По́льша	по-по́льски	
Росси́я	по-ру́сски	
Испа́ния	по-испа́нски	
Украйна	по-украйнски	
Еги́пет	по-ара́бски	
Кита́й	по-кита́йски	Азия
Япо́ния	по-япо́нски	

How do you speak? Как вы говори́те?

well	хорошо́	not very well	не о́чень хорошо́
quite well	дово́льно хорошо́	a bit	немно́жко
very well	о́чень хорошо́	badly	пло́хо

6. More sums

Ask each other questions with numbers.
Answers not higher than 100.

Два́дцать два плюс два́дцать два? - Со́рок четы́ре!
Три́дцать ми́нус оди́ннадцать? - Девятна́дцать!
Со́рок два плюс три́дцать три? -
Девяно́сто шесть ми́нус шестна́дцать? -

23 + 18?
59 - 34?
77 + 12?
и т.д.

THE NEW YEAR AND CHRISTMAS

Russian winter celebrations do not start until the New Year, when they have a New Year Fir Tree and champagne at midnight. New Year's Day is the day for children's presents, which are delivered by Father Frost and his little helper, Snegurochka the Snow Maiden. There is a long public holiday, and Christmas, according to the Orthodox calendar, is celebrated on January 7th. It is a religious festival with midnight mass in the churches.

The "Old New Year" (New Year according to the old Orthodox calendar) is also celebrated on January 13th!

"С Но́вым Го́дом!"
"Happy New Year!"

New Year	Но́вый Го́д
New Year tree	ёлка
champagne	шампа́нское
presents	пода́рки
Father Frost	Дед Моро́з
Snegurochka	Снегу́рочка
Christmas	Рождество́
Old New Year	Ста́рый Но́вый Го́д

"Happy New Year!" "С Но́вым го́дом!"
"Happy Christmas!" "С Рождество́м!"
(These are instrumental endings. See lesson 10.)

LESSON 5 ГОСТИНИЦА УРОК 5

Ivan checks in to the Hotel Mars, finds his room, and telephones Lyudmila to invite her out.

In this lesson you will:

❑ learn some of the words you will need if you stay in a Russian hotel.
❑ learn how to ask whether places are open.
❑ learn the days of the week.

The grammar includes:

❑ the short form of adjectives.
❑ the use of с with the genitive meaning "from".
❑ the present tense of the verb говори́ть - "to speak".
❑ a note on the use of imperfective and perfective verb aspects.
❑ the use of у меня́ and у вас to convey "I have" and "you have".

There is practice filling in the form upon arrival at a Russian hotel, and there is information on Russian hotels and on GUM - ГУМ - the former State Universal Shop.

The **Ruslan 1 Workbook** contains 16 additional exercises for this lesson, including 3 listening exercises.
In the **Ruslan 1 Reader**, Igor is on a business trip to Novosibirsk.
The **Ruslan 1 CD Rom** contains 28 additional exercises with sound, including a video exercise.

Гости́ница "Ба́лчуг" в це́нтре Москвы́

РЕСТОРАН
Оплата только в рублях
Мест НЕТ
ОБМЕН ВАЛЮТЫ
КАССА
ПОЧТА
Закрыто на обед
Телефон не работает
БАР
ПЕПСИ КОЛА!
ЛИФТ
АДМИНИСТРАТОР
Оплата только в рублях
СУВЕНИРЫ

41/46

Ива́н в гости́нице "Марс"

Ива́н: Здра́вствуйте!
Администра́тор: Я вас слу́шаю.
Ива́н: Мо́жно заказа́ть но́мер?
Администра́тор: Сейча́с... да, мо́жно. Вы оди́н?
Ива́н: Да, оди́н. До пя́тницы мо́жно?
Администра́тор: До пя́тницы? Да, э́то мо́жно. Запо́лните э́тот бланк.

42/47

He fills in the form

Ива́н: Вот, пожа́луйста.
Администра́тор: Хорошо́. Вы из Сара́нска, да? Вот ключ. Ва́ша ко́мната но́мер два́дцать пять. Это нале́во. У вас есть бага́ж?
Ива́н: Да, вот: чемода́н и су́мка. Скажи́те, в но́мере есть телефо́н?
Администра́тор: Коне́чно, всё есть. Телефо́н, телеви́зор, душ.
Ива́н: И всё рабо́тает?
Администра́тор: Вот э́то я не зна́ю.
Ива́н: А рестора́н есть в гости́нице?
Администра́тор: Да, рестора́н и буфе́т. В рестора́не есть бар.
Ива́н: Бар сейча́с откры́т?
Администра́тор: Нет. Он закры́т. Сейча́с уже́ по́здно.
Ива́н: Как жаль! А когда́ рабо́тает рестора́н?
Администра́тор: Рестора́н сейча́с то́же закры́т, а за́втра он откры́т с ча́са.
Ива́н: Спаси́бо. Мо́жно заказа́ть чай?
Администра́тор: Мо́жно, коне́чно. До за́втра.

43/48

Типи́чный англича́нин

Англича́нин: Мо́жно заказа́ть биле́т в Большо́й теа́тр?
Администра́тор: Коне́чно, но то́лько за́втра. Сего́дня ка́сса уже́ закры́та.
Англича́нин: Хорошо́, я понима́ю, спаси́бо. А где магази́н ГУМ?
Администра́тор: ГУМ в це́нтре, напро́тив Кремля́.
Англича́нин: Спаси́бо.

44/49

In his hotel room Ivan telephones Zoya Petrovna

Ива́н: Алло́!... Зо́я Петро́вна? Извини́те, что я так по́здно... А... Лю́да у вас? ... Да, е́сли мо́жно.

Ива́н: Лю́да, я приглаша́ю вас за́втра в рестора́н. Как вы на э́то смо́трите? ... Хорошо́?! ... Ну, прекра́сно! Тогда́ здесь, в гости́нице, в час. ... Что? ... Да, рестора́н в гости́нице. До свида́ния. До за́втра.

A knock at the door

45/50

Ива́н: Да?
Дежу́рная: Прости́те, вот ваш чай.
Ива́н: Спаси́бо.
Дежу́рная: Пожа́луйста.
Ива́н: Скажи́те, у вас тарака́ны есть?
Дежу́рная: Коне́чно, нет!

www

администра́тор	administrator
я вас слу́шаю	I'm listening to you (ready to serve you)
заказа́ть (perf.)	to book
но́мер	hotel room, number
оди́н	on your own
пя́тница	Friday
запо́лнить (perf.)	to fill in
бланк	form
ключ	key
У вас есть?	Do you have?
телеви́зор	TV set
душ	shower
всё	everything
буфе́т	snack bar
бар	bar
за́втра	tomorrow
откры́т	open
закры́т	closed
по́здно	late
Как жаль!	What a pity!
когда́	when
час	1 o'clock
с (+ gen.)	from
с ча́са	from 1 o'clock
ка́сса	booking office, cash desk
магази́н	shop
напро́тив (+ gen.)	opposite
кремль (m.)	kremlin
Алло́!	Hello! (on the phone)
е́сли	if
приглаша́ть	to invite
смотре́ть	to look at
Как вы на э́то смо́трите?	What do you think of that?
тогда́	then / in that case
До свида́ния!	Goodbye!
дежу́рная	lady on duty
тарака́ны	cockroaches

www **ГУМ - Госуда́рственный Универса́льный Магази́н**

The former "State Universal Shop" has been completely changed since perestroika. Previously it was an enormous centrally organised department store. Now it is divided into sections, which are leased out to high class Russian and Western retailers.

Гости́ницы - Hotels in Russia

Accommodation normally has to be booked before you travel to Russia, as part of the visa application process. Usually such bookings are made in Western-style hotels.

If you stay in a Russian-style hotel, be ready to pay on arrival. In a Russian hotel, the **администра́тор** looks after the reception desk. The **дежу́рная** is the lady who looks after your floor, usually with a table on the landing.

www **Кремль**

This means "fortress". The Kremlin is not unique to Moscow. There is a kremlin in several old Russian towns and cities.

Моско́вский Кремль и Москва́-река́

Days of the week

Monday	понеде́льник
Tuesday	вто́рник
Wednesday	среда́
Thursday	четве́рг
Friday	пя́тница
Saturday	суббо́та
Sunday	воскресе́нье

The Russians use small letters for the days of the week.

ГРАММАТИКА

www **До за́втра! - Till tomorrow!**

сего́дня - today   за́втра - tomorrow   вчера́ - yesterday

These three words never change their endings.

Short adjectives

Short adjectives are used in sentences like "The restaurant is closed".
They agree with the noun they are describing as follows:

Masculine:	Рестора́н закры́т.	The restaurant is closed.
Feminine:	Ка́сса была́ откры́та.	The cash desk was open.
Neuter:	Бюро закрыто.	The office is shut.

Рестора́н откры́т с ча́са. The restaurant is open from 1 o'clock.

The word "с" has two meanings. Here it means "from" and takes the genitive case. For example:

с ча́са - from 1 o'clock
с пя́тницы - from Friday

Use с for "from" for times, and also for places that use на for "to" (lesson 2). www
For places that use в for "to" use из for "from".
In lesson 10 you will meet с meaning "with", taking the instrumental case.

говори́ть - "to speak" or "to say" - a second conjugation verb:

я говорю́	I speak	мы говори́м	we speak
ты говори́шь	you speak (familiar)	вы говори́те	you speak (polite or plural)
он / она́ говори́т	he / she speaks	они́ говоря́т	they speak

For the conjugation of **смотре́ть** (another second conjugation verb which has stress changes) and for other examples, see the verb review, page 134.

Verb aspects - warning not to use perfective verbs yet!

Most Russian verbs have two infinitives, one imperfective and the other perfective. These are called "aspects".

The verbs that you have used so far for the present tense - e.g. **знать**, **рабо́тать**, **смотре́ть** - have all been in the imperfective aspect.

You have also met several perfective verbs. These are used for single actions and so far you have met them in the past tense or in the infinitive only.
For example, **заказа́ть** - "to order", **останови́ться** - "to stay" or "to stop".
Do not try to use these perfective verbs to form the present tense. In "Ruslan 2" you will use them to form the future perfective tense.

у меня́ есть, у вас есть

There is no commonly used verb "to have" in Russian. They say instead: "In the possession of me / of you there is":

У вас есть бага́ж?	Do you have any luggage?
У меня́ есть су́мка.	I have a bag.
У Ива́на есть телефо́н.	Ivan has a phone.
У Людми́лы есть секре́т.	Lyudmila has a secret.

Often есть is left out, and the word order can be reversed:

Биле́т у меня́.	I have the ticket

For the past tense use был / была́ / бы́ло / бы́ли:

У меня́ была́ командиро́вка.	I had a business trip.
У Игоря была́ жена́.	Igor had a wife.

1. Answer the questions on the dialogues

а. Ива́н заказа́л но́мер в гости́нице “Ба́лчуг”?
б. В но́мере Ива́на есть телефо́н?
в. Телефо́н рабо́тает?
г. В гости́нице есть рестора́н?
д. Бар был откры́т?
е. Рестора́н был откры́т?
ж. Гости́ница была́ откры́та?
з. Ива́н заказа́л ко́фе?

2. Fill in the gaps

а. Ива́н __________ в гости́нице.
б. В но́мере ________ телефо́н.
в. Рестора́н __________ с ча́са.
г. В гости́нице ка́сса __________ .
д. Ива́н ________ чай.
е. Вы __________ телеви́зор.
ж. Телефо́н в но́мере не __________ .
з. Администра́тор __________ на бага́ж.

закры́та
заказа́л
есть
был
смо́трит
рабо́тает
откры́т
смо́трите

3. Fill the gaps in the phone conversation

Я вас ______________ в рестора́н.
Очень __________! А когда́?
За́втра, в __________ .
Хорошо́! А __________ ?
Здесь в _____________ в ____________ .

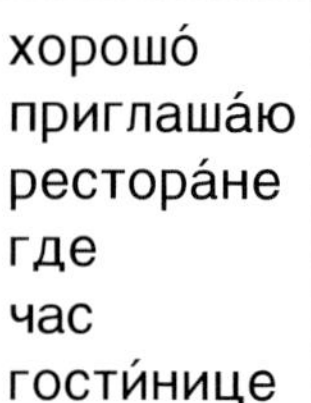

4. Put the sentences into the present tense

а. Ива́н смотре́л телеви́зор. ____________________________
б. Бар был закры́т. ____________________________
в. Зо́я Петро́вна была́ в рестора́не. ____________________________
г. Ка́сса была́ закры́та. ____________________________
д. Людми́ла рабо́тала в Москве́. ____________________________
е. Мы зна́ли Санкт-Петербу́рг. ____________________________
ж. Они не понима́ли. ____________________________

You have arrived at the Hotel “Марс”. Fill in the registration form in Russian handwriting

www

ГОСТИНИЦА МАРС - АНКЕТА ГОСТЯ

Фамилия ______________

Имя ______________

Отчество ______________

Адрес:

Почтовый индекс ______________

Город ______________

Улица ______________

Дом ______________

Гражданство ______________

Профессия ______________

Дата рождения ______________

Место рождения ______________

Номер паспорта ______________

Цель приезда ______________

Место ______________

Число ______________

Подпись ______________

анкéта	questionnaire
гость (m.)	guest
óтчество	patronymic
почтóвый и́ндекс	post code
гóрод	town
дом	house
граждáнство	nationality
профéссия	occupation
дáта	date
рождéние	birth
мéсто	place
цель (f.)	purpose
приéзд	arrival / visit
числó	date
пóдпись (f.)	signature

СЛУШАЙТЕ!  УРОК 5

51

Ivan phones his Moscow boss

1. What is the name of Ivan's boss?
2. When did Ivan arrive from London?
3. Where is the hotel "Марс"?
4. Does Ivan know where to go tomorrow?
5. What does Ivan's boss write down?

ГОВОРИТЕ И ПИШИТЕ!

1. Make up sentences about where people work

Профе́ссии	**Места́ рабо́ты**
профе́ссор	теа́тр
медсестра́	больни́ца
учи́тель	цирк
арти́ст	такси́
секрета́рь	газе́та
президе́нт	Кремль
кло́ун	бюро́
журнали́ст	шко́ла
шофёр	университе́т

The first one has been done for you.

Note that when you say "in the Kremlin" the stress moves to the end of the word: в Кремле́.
Note the two alternative ways of writing the letter "т": *m*/*т*
(Here we have used the first).

Артист работает в театре.

1. Role-play. A hotel guest and the receptionist

Ask if you can book a room.	Yes, of course.
Ask about a telephone, television, shower, and whether they are working.	Make up your own answers.
Is the restaurant open?	No, it's closed.
Is the bar open?	No, it's closed.
Ask if you can order tea.	Yes, of course.

2. Communication game for a group

A variation on bingo. Everyone has the same list of places in the town:

Ресторáн - Кáсса - Банк - Музéй
Поликли́ника - Гости́ница - Теáтр

The teacher decides which places are open. At least three.

The learners tick three places on their list that they would like to go to. Then take turns asking questions, and see who can find the most open places:

- Скажи́те, пожáлуйста, банк откры́т?
- Нет, банк закры́т.
- Как жаль!

- Поликли́ника откры́та?
- Да. Откры́та.
- Хорошó, спаси́бо.

Once learners are used to this activity, it can be played in smaller groups and learners can take the place of the teacher.

LESSON 6	РЕСТОРАН	УРОК 6

Ivan and Lyudmila are in the restaurant of the hotel "Mars". Just as they are starting their meal, who should arrive but Vadim with a new companion!

You will learn:

- ❑ how to order a meal in a Russian restaurant.
- ❑ words for food and drink.

You will learn the following grammatical points:

- ❑ the verbs
  хоте́ть - to want
  идти́ - to go by foot.
- ❑ the endings of neuter nouns.
- ❑ the accusative case, used for the object of a verb.
- ❑ adjectives in the nominative case.
- ❑ the word for "which" - како́й.

The information sections are on the great Russian poet A.S. Pushkin and on Russian food, and at the end of the lesson there is an old Russian folk song "The Steppe all around".

By the end of the lesson you should be able to:

- ❑ find what you want from a Russian menu.
- ❑ order a meal.

The **Ruslan 1 Workbook** contains 18 additional exercises for this lesson, including 3 listening exercises.
In the **Ruslan 1 Reader**, Igor and Nellie visit a restaurant in Novosibirsk and there is a quiz with pictures of Russian dishes.
The **Ruslan 1 CD Rom** contains 27 additional exercises with sound, including a video exercise.

Блины́, вода́, вино́, во́дка и ры́ба!
Pancakes, water, wine, vodka and fish!

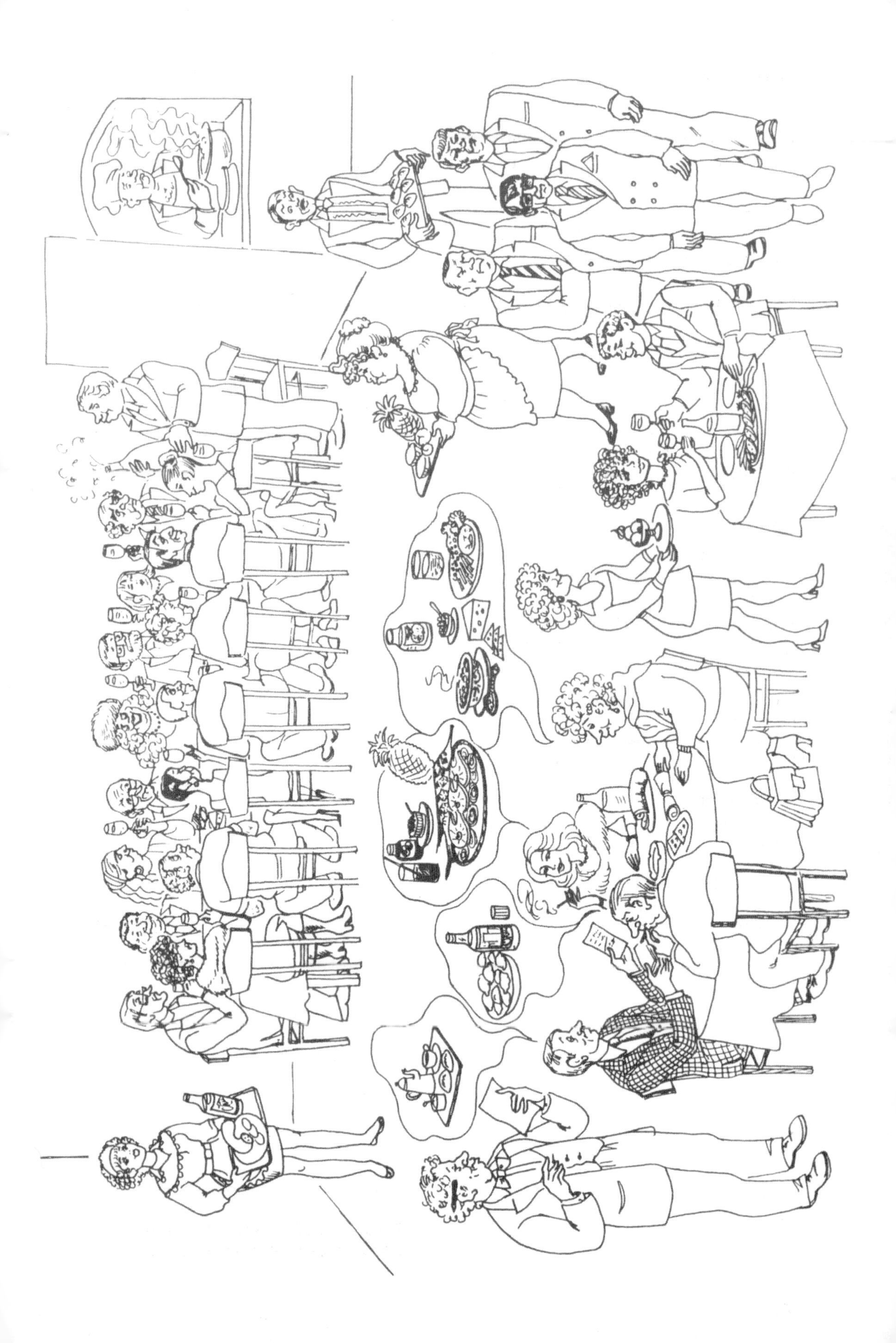

53

В рестора́не

Ива́н: Здра́вствуйте, Людми́ла.
Людми́ла: Здра́вствуйте.
Ива́н: Проходи́те, пожа́луйста. Хоро́ший рестора́н, пра́вда? Вот свобо́дный сто́лик. Сади́тесь, пожа́луйста.
Людми́ла: Ива́н, вы хорошо́ зна́ете Москву́?
Ива́н: Коне́чно. А вот и официа́нтка! Де́вушка! ...
Официа́нтка: Мину́точку!

54

Меню́

Ива́н: Де́вушка, мо́жно посмотре́ть меню́?
Официа́нтка: Вот, пожа́луйста, меню́.
Ива́н: Так... заку́ски: моско́вский сала́т, кра́сная и чёрная икра́, колбаса́, сыр. Напи́тки: пи́во, во́дка, вино́, минера́льная вода́.... Людми́ла, что вы хоти́те? ...

55

Напи́тки и заку́ски

Ива́н: Де́вушка, да́йте буты́лку во́дки и буты́лку пи́ва.
Людми́ла: А вино́ у вас есть?
Официа́нтка: Коне́чно.
Людми́ла: Како́е у вас вино́?
Официа́нтка: Кра́сное и бе́лое.
Людми́ла: Принеси́те мне бе́лое вино́.
Ива́н: Да-да, коне́чно, принеси́те бе́лое вино́. А ско́лько сто́ит икра́? Ого́! Икра́ о́чень дорога́я!
Людми́ла: Принеси́те мне, пожа́луйста, икру́...
Ива́н: А мне сыр, и чёрный хлеб.
Людми́ла: А мне бе́лый хлеб, пожа́луйста..
Официа́нтка: Это всё?
Ива́н: Да, э́то всё.

56

Инти́мный вопро́с

Ива́н: Людми́ла, тепе́рь, пока́ мы одни́, мо́жно зада́ть вам оди́н инти́мный вопро́с? У вас есть Русла́н?
Людми́ла: Что? Русла́н? Почему́ вы спра́шиваете?
Ива́н: Потому́, что мне о́чень интере́сно.
Людми́ла: Я не понима́ю. Смотри́те кто там... Вади́м!
Ива́н: Вади́м... и не оди́н!
Вади́м: Лю́дочка! Прия́тного аппети́та! Что ты здесь де́лаешь? Како́й сюрпри́з! ... И Ива́н Никола́евич, вы то́же здесь!
Ива́н: Да, я то́же здесь. Здра́вствуйте, Вади́м Бори́сович, сади́тесь.
Вади́м: Да нет, спаси́бо, мне пора́, я не оди́н. Мы идём на о́перу. До свида́ния, Лю́да.

Типи́чный англича́нин:

57

Англича́нин:	Извини́те, вы говори́те по-англи́йски?
Официа́нтка:	Нет.
Англича́нин:	Извини́те, что тако́е борщ?
Официа́нтка:	Это суп.
Англича́нин:	А что тако́е щи?
Официа́нтка:	Это то́же суп.
Англича́нин:	Хорошо́. Да́йте, пожа́луйста, моско́вский сала́т!

хоро́ший	good
пра́вда	truth
пра́вда?	isn't it?
свобо́дный	free (in the sense of "vacant")
сто́лик	small table
Сади́тесь!	Sit down!
официа́нтка	waitress
де́вушка	young lady (used to call the waitress)
Мину́точку!	Just a minute!
посмотре́ть (perf.)	to have a look
меню́	menu
моско́вский	Moscow (adj.)
кра́сный	red
чёрный	black
хоте́ть	to want
Да́йте!	Give (me / us)!
буты́лка	bottle
како́й	what sort of / which
бе́лый	white
Принеси́те!	Bring (me / us)!
ско́лько?	how much?
сто́ить	to cost
Ско́лько сто́ит?	How much does it cost?
дорого́й	dear / expensive
тепе́рь	now
пока́	while
мы одни́	we are alone
зада́ть вопро́с (perf.)	to ask a question
инти́мный	intimate

почему́	why
потому́ что	because
спра́шивать	to ask
пора́	it's time ...
Мне пора́.	It's time for me (to go)
Прия́тного аппети́та!	Enjoy (your) meal! (the "г" is pronounced "v")
идти́	to go (by foot)
о́пера	opera
Что тако́е ...?	What is ...?

Vocabulary for the food items is listed separately on page 77.

Пи́во "Ба́лтика"
"Baltika" beer

"Руслáн и Людми́ла"
This is the title of a famous poem by A.S. Pushkin (1799-1837). It is a love story, set in a mystical kingdom, where the hero Руслáн goes through numerous adventures in order to save the girl he loves, Людми́ла, from evil forces. Eventually real love overcomes evil and they are united.
Ивáн is referring to this story when he asks Людми́ла:

"У вас есть Руслáн?"

www **Alexander Sergeyevich Pushkin** is revered in Russia as the greatest Russian poet, and his works are very popular. The first lines of "Руслáн и Людми́ла" are well known by Russian children:

www

У лукомóрья дуб зелёный;	By the seashore there is a green oak;
Златáя цепь на ду́бе том:	There is a golden chain on that oak:
И днём и нóчью кот учёный	And day and night a learned cat
Всё хóдит по цепи́ кругóм;	Walks round and round on the chain;
Идёт напрáво - песнь завóдит,	He goes to the right - and sings a song,
Налéво - скáзку говори́т.	To the left - and tells a fairy tale.

ГРАММАТИКА

Вот свобóдный стóлик. There is a free table.
The word "free" in English has several meanings. In Russian "free" in the sense of "vacant" or "having freedom" is свобóдный, while "free of charge" is бесплáтный.

хотéть - "to want" - an irregular verb
я хочу́, ты хóчешь, он / онá хóчет, мы хоти́м, вы хоти́те, они хотя́т

идти́ - "to go" (by foot)
я иду́, ты идёшь, он / онá идёт, мы идём, вы идёте, они иду́т

For "to go" (by transport) use éхать:
я éду, ты éдешь, он / онá éдет, мы éдем, вы éдете, они́ éдут

Дáйте ... ! - Give (me / us) ... !
This is the imperative of the perfective verb дать - "to give".
Дáйте москóвский салáт! Give me a Moscow salad!

Принеси́те ... ! - Bring (me / us) ... !
This is the imperative of the perfective verb принести́ - "to bring".
Принеси́те, пожáлуйста, кóфе! Bring me a coffee, please!

Neuter nouns

We saw in lesson 2 that neuter nouns usually end in -о or -е:

вино́ - wine
мо́ре - the sea

Most neuter noun endings are the same as those of masculine nouns.
For example the usual genitive singular ending is -а or -я:

вина́ - of wine
мо́ря - of the sea

The neuter form of мой is моё and of ваш is ва́ше

Где моё пи́во?	Where is my beer?	Вот оно́!	There it is!
Это ва́ше вино́?	Is this your wine?	Да, моё.	Yes, it's mine.

The accusative case

The accusative case is used for the direct object of a verb.
Inanimate masculine and neuter nouns stay the same.
Feminine nouns change -а to -у, -я to -ю and -ия to -ию.
Feminine nouns in -ь stay the same.

Вы зна́ете Ло́ндон?	Do you know London?
Вы зна́ете Москву́?	Do you know Moscow?
Да́йте буты́лку во́дки!	Give (us) a bottle of vodka!
Он хорошо́ зна́ет Росси́ю.	He knows Russia well.
Я люблю́ мо́ре.	I love the sea.

The case endings are used even when the verb is left out:

Мне икру́!	(Bring) the caviare for me!

The accusative is also used with в or на meaning "to" a place

It answers the question куда́? - "where to?" (Lesson 7).

Куда́ вы идёте?	Where are you going?
Я иду́ в рестора́н.	I am going to the restaurant.
Мы идём на о́перу.	We are going to the opera.
Она́ е́дет в Росси́ю.	She is going to Russia.

Adjectives in the nominative case

Adjectives agree with the nouns they describe.
Nominative adjective endings are:

Masculine	-ый, -ий or -о́й	-о́й is always stressed.
Feminine	-ая or -яя	The soft ending -яя is quite rare.
Neuter	-ое or -ее	The soft ending -ее is quite rare.

Большо́й теа́тр - the Bolshoy (big) theatre
моско́вский сала́т - Moscow salad
чёрный хлеб - black bread
кра́сная икра́ - red caviare
бе́лое вино́ - white wine

како́й - кака́я - како́е

како́й is an adjective meaning "what" or "which".

Како́й вопро́с?	What question?
Кака́я прия́тная встре́ча!	What a pleasant meeting!

УПРАЖНЕНИЯ УРОК 6

1. Choose the correct answers

а.	Ива́н ду́мает, что рестора́н хоро́ший?	Да / Нет
б.	В рестора́не есть вино́?	Да / Нет
в.	Икра́ дорога́я?	Да / Нет
г.	Кто хо́чет икру́? Ива́н и́ли Людми́ла?	Ива́н / Людми́ла
д.	Кто хо́чет сыр? Ива́н и́ли Людми́ла?	Ива́н / Людми́ла
е.	Како́й хлеб хо́чет Ива́н?	Бе́лый / Чёрный
ж.	Како́й хлеб хо́чет Людми́ла?	Бе́лый / Чёрный
з.	Вади́м оди́н и́ли не оди́н?	Оди́н / Не оди́н

2. Fill in the gaps in the dialogue

- _________, вот Вади́м!
- А что он здесь _________?
- Я не _________, что он де́лает.
- А он не _________!
- Да, _________ не оди́н!
- _________ сюрпри́з!
- Прия́тного ____________

де́лает
оди́н
он
Смотри́те
аппети́та!
Како́й
зна́ю

3. Gap fill. Change the ending if necessary

- Что вы хоти́те?
- Я хочу́ _________ и _________ (сала́т / вино́)
- А я хочу́ _______, _______, и _______. (икра́ / хлеб / во́дка)
- Я хочу́ ________, и _________ вина́. (икра́ / буты́лка)
- Я тоже хочу́ _________. (вино́)
- Хорошо́! Де́вушка, принеси́те, пожа́луйста,

__________, __________, __________, __________,

__________, __________ и __________.

ЧИТАЙТЕ!

1. Make a note in Russian of what you would choose from the menu opposite.

____

____

____

58

МЕНЮ

ЗАКУСКИ
Икра красная
Икра чёрная
Салат московский
Колбаса
Сыр голландский

ПЕРВЫЕ БЛЮДА
Борщ
Щи
Окрошка
Солянка

ВТОРЫЕ БЛЮДА
Бефстроганов
Котлеты по-киевски
Сибирские пельмени
Осетрина заливная
Шашлык
Цыплёнок жареный

СЛАДКИЕ БЛЮДА
Мороженое
Салат фруктовый
Ананас

ГОРЯЧИЕ НАПИТКИ
Чай
Кофе

НАПИТКИ
Сок яблочный
Сок томатный
Красное вино
Белое вино
Шампанское
Пиво “Жигулёвское”
Водка “Столичная”

ананáс	pineapple
бефстрóганов	beef Stroganoff
борщ	beetroot soup
винó	wine
водá	water
вóдка	vodka
вторы́е блю́да	second dishes (the main course)
голлáндский	Dutch
горя́чий	hot
жáреный	roasted
“Жигулёвское”	brand of beer
закýски	hors d’oeuvre
заливнóй	in aspic
икрá	caviare
квас	drink made from rye bread or black bread
кефи́р	thin yoghurt
колбасá	salami
котлéты	meatballs
крáсный	red
минерáльный	mineral
морóженое	ice cream
москóвский	Moscow (adj.)
напи́тки	drinks
окрóшка	clear soup (cold, made with kvas or kefir)
осетри́на	sturgeon
пельмéни	pelmeny (like small stuffed dumplings)
пéрвые блю́да	first dishes (usually soups)
пи́во	beer
по-ки́евски	Kiev fashion
салáт	salad
сиби́рский	Siberian
слáдкий	sweet
сок	juice
соля́нка	soup with ingredients that include pickled or salted vegetables
“Столи́чная”	brand of vodka
суп	soup
сыр	cheese
томáтный	tomato (adj.)
фруктóвый	fruit (adj.)
хлеб	bread
цыплёнок	young chicken
чай	tea
шампáнское	champagne
шашлы́к	shashlyk
щи	cabbage soup
я́блочный	apple (adj.)

Russian Food

The usual daily meals are: **за́втрак** - breakfast.

обе́д - the midday meal, main meal of the day, often as late as 2 or 3pm.

у́жин - the evening meal.

Soup - **суп** - is an important element of the main meal, and is served all year round. **Борщ** (beetroot soup) and **щи** (cabbage soup) are well known in the West, but apart from these there is a wide variety of other types of soup, including cold summer soups.

A celebration meal starts with **заку́ски** (hors d'oeuvre), for example salads, cold meat and fish dishes, pickles and **пиро́г** (pie) or **пирожки́** (small savory pies). This is followed by the main hot meat or fish dish. The dessert is often fruit or ice cream. Tea, often with lemon, is usually served at the end of the meal.

If vodka is drunk, it is not normal to sip your glass. It is more usual to drink only when someone in the group makes a toast.

Russian champagne - **шампа́нское** - is a sparkling white wine.

If you are a vegetarian - **вегетариа́нец** / **вегетариа́нка** - then life can be difficult, although in summer Russian salads are excellent.

Reading the menu

In menus the adjectives are normally printed after the nouns, but when you talk about the item you put the adjective in front in the normal way.

You read: "Сала́т моско́вский".
You say: "Моско́вский сала́т".

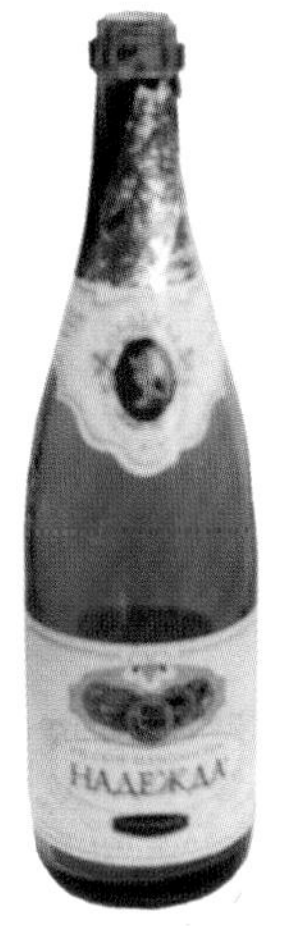

Шампа́нское "Наде́жда"

СЛУШАЙТЕ!

59 **Vadim is having a meal with his new acquaintance Vera**

1. Why doesn't Vera want caviare?
2. What does Vera want to drink?
3. Name two items that Vadim ordered.
4. What do Vadim and Vera think of this restaurant?

ГОВОРИТЕ! УРОК 6

1. **Role-play (for pair work)**
   You are with your partner in the restaurant of the Hotel Марс.

Say it is a good restaurant.	Agree.
Suggest looking at the menu.	Agree.

Use the menu on page 77, and decide together what you want to eat.

Order your meal from your teacher or another learner who plays the part of the waiter.

2. **Game in a circle to practise the verb хоте́ть**
   Stand in a circle of not more than 6 people. The first says what he or she wants to eat or drink from the menu on page 77:

Пи́тер: Я хочу́ бефстро́ганов

The next person in the circle repeats this in the third person, and then says what he or she wants:

Ни́на: Пи́тер хо́чет бефстро́ганов, а я хочу́ икру́.

The next person adds on another item, and so on until you have been round the whole ring. At this stage you will probably have to help each other.

As a variant you can go back to the beginning if anyone makes a mistake in the Russian.

Then everyone in the circle moves round and talks to every one else in turn, trying to remember what they want:

- Вы хоти́те бефстро́ганов, да?
- Да, а вы хоти́те борщ?
- Нет, я хочу́ щи.
- А я хочу́ пельме́ни!

Сиби́рские пельме́ни

ГОВОРИТЕ!

3. Pair up the nouns and adjectives

хлеб винó ресторáн центр кни́га теáтр салáт буты́лка стóлик билéт	бéлый крáсный большóй москóвский нóвый дорогóй инти́мный коммéрческий индустриáльный свобóдный

One member of the group calls out a noun from the left hand box. Others then have to find adjectives that will go with the chosen noun to make sense, and read them out with the correct ending.

- Буты́лка!
  - Большáя буты́лка!
  - Нóвая буты́лка!
  - Дорогáя буты́лка!

4. Food from different countries

Collect packets and cans or pictures of food from different countries. Then ask questions about them.

- Это францу́зский сыр?
- Да. Это францу́зский сыр.

- Это францу́зское винó?
- Нет. Это испáнское винó.

- Где италья́нское винó?
- Вот онó!

американский
англи́йский
голлáндский
гречéский
грузи́нский
испáнский
итальянский
китáйский
немéцкий
пóльский
ру́сский
украинский
францу́зский
япóнский

Китáйский ресторáн

СТЕПЬ ДА СТЕПЬ КРУГОМ

97

Степь да степь кругóм,
Путь далёк лежи́т.
В той степи́ глухóй
Умирáл ямщи́к.

И набрáвшись сил,
Чýя смéрти час,
Он товáрищу
Отдавáл накáз.

Ты, товáрищ мой,
Не попóмни зла.
Здесь в степи́ глухóй
Схорони́ меня́.

А женé скажи́,
Что в степи́ замёрз,
А любóвь её
Я с собóй унёс.

Степь да степь кругóм,
Путь далёк лежи́т.
В той степи́ глухóй
Умирáл ямщи́к.

THE STEPPE ALL AROUND

The steppe is all around,
The distant road ahead.
In that distant steppe
The coachman was dying.

And gathering his strength,
Sensing the hour of death.
To his comrade
He made a request.

You, my friend
Forget our difficulties.
Here in the distant steppe
Bury me.

And tell my wife
That I froze in the steppe.
And her love
I took away with me.

The steppe is all around,
The distant road ahead.
In that distant steppe
The coachman was dying.

This old Russian folk song is the last track on the Ruslan 1 audio CD. It is sung by the Rossica choir, who recorded the dialogues in this book. You can obtain their CD of Russian traditional and religious songs from Ruslan Limited: www.ruslan.co.uk/other.htm

Ivan and Lyudmila are still in the restaurant, and start talking about their lives and interests. Lyudmila has to leave when things get serious, and Ivan hurries to pay the bill.

This lesson includes:

- ❑ neuter forms of verbs.
- ❑ the preposition о meaning "about", which takes the prepositional case.
- ❑ more nouns ending in a soft sign. These can be masculine or feminine.
- ❑ nouns ending in -мя. These are neuter.
- ❑ how to form impersonal expressions and adverbs from adjectives: интере́сно - "it is interesting".
- ❑ numbers above 100.

There is information on the river Volga.

By the end of the lesson you should be able to:

- ❑ say something about what you like doing in your free time.
- ❑ talk about the town / area in which you live.

At this stage you should thoroughly revise the verbs you have met so far in this course. See the verb review, pages 134 and 135.

> The **Ruslan 1 Workbook** contains 18 additional exercises for this lesson, including 5 listening exercises.
> In the **Ruslan 1 Reader** there is a text about Nellie's life in Novosibirsk, and a song for learners - "Люблю́ я борщ".
> The **Ruslan 1 CD Rom** contains 30 additional exercises with sound.

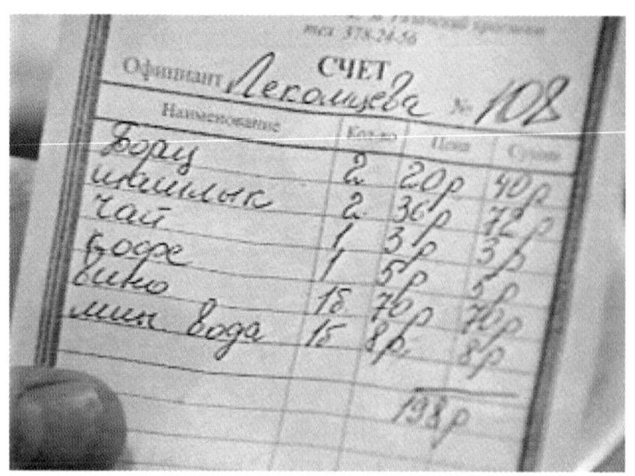

Счёт - The bill

301

61/65

Lyudmila and Ivan are finishing their lunch in the restaurant

Ива́н: Лю́да, у вас тако́е краси́вое и́мя - Людми́ла!... А как обе́д?
Людми́ла: Ничего́, спаси́бо. Рестора́н действи́тельно хоро́ший.
Ива́н: Лю́да, расскажи́те мне о себе́: где вы живёте, где рабо́таете? Почему́ вы живёте у Вади́ма? Кто он вам? Мо́жет быть, он ваш "Русла́н"?
Людми́ла: Нет. Снача́ла расскажи́те о себе́.
Ива́н: Вы уже́ всё обо мне зна́ете: я живу́ и рабо́таю в Сара́нске.
Людми́ла: Вы действи́тельно миллионе́р?
Ива́н: Ну, не зна́ю... Почему́ вы так ду́маете?
Людми́ла: Потому́ что Вади́м говори́л, что у вас мно́го де́нег.
Ива́н: Ах, Вади́м говори́л! Ну, э́то не интере́сно. Расскажи́те о себе́. Что вы лю́бите де́лать в свобо́дное вре́мя?
Людми́ла: Я люблю́ ходи́ть в кино́, в теа́тр, смотре́ть телеви́зор, слу́шать му́зыку... люблю́ чита́ть.
Ива́н: А что вы лю́бите чита́ть? Вы лю́бите чита́ть о любви́?
Людми́ла: Ива́н. Не на́до.

62/66

Ива́н: А тепе́рь расскажи́те о Вади́ме.
Людми́ла: Вади́м изве́стный кинокри́тик. Вы не чита́ли его́ кни́гу?
Ива́н: Нет, не чита́л.
Людми́ла: Это интере́сный челове́к. Он ча́сто приглаша́ет меня́ в Дом кино́.
Ива́н: И э́то всё?
Людми́ла: Я же вам говорю́: мы ча́сто хо́дим в кино́ и в теа́тр вме́сте. И э́то всё. Тепе́рь расскажи́те о Сара́нске. Это на Во́лге?
Ива́н: Нет, Сара́нск не на Во́лге, но э́то не о́чень далеко́ от Во́лги. Дово́льно большо́й индустриа́льный го́род. Столи́ца Мордо́вии.
Людми́ла: А что там мо́жно де́лать?
Ива́н: Как и везде́: ходи́ть в кино́ и в теа́тр, смотре́ть телеви́зор, чита́ть, говори́ть о любви́...
Людми́ла: Ну, мне пора́! Уже по́здно. Спаси́бо за вку́сный обе́д.
Ива́н: Лю́да, куда́ вы идёте?
Людми́ла: Нет-нет, мне пора́, я иду́ домо́й...
Ива́н: Хорошо́. Пойдёмте!

63/67

Ivan pays the bill

Ива́н: Де́вушка! Да́йте, пожа́луйста, счёт.
Официа́нтка: Вот, пожа́луйста.
Ива́н: Ого́! Вот э́то да! Инфля́ция! Три́ста три́дцать рубле́й. Хорошо́. Три́ста и три́дцать.
Официа́нтка: Спаси́бо.
Ива́н: Пожа́луйста.

Типи́чный англича́нин

64

Англича́нин:	Извини́те, у меня́ суп холо́дный.
Официа́нтка:	Да, холо́дный.
Англича́нин:	А что де́лать?
Официа́нтка:	Како́й у вас суп? Окро́шка?
Англича́нин:	Да. А что?
Официа́нтка:	Она́ всегда́ холо́дная!

краси́вый	beautiful
и́мя (n.)	first name
обе́д	lunch / meal
действи́тельно	really
рассказа́ть (perf.)	to tell
о себе́	about oneself
жить	to live
снача́ла	at first
пото́м	then
так	in this way
мно́го	a lot
де́ньги	money
де́нег	of money
люби́ть	to love
вре́мя (n.)	time
ходи́ть	to go (by foot, regularly)
чита́ть	to read
слу́шать	to listen to
му́зыка	music
любо́вь (f.)	love
о любви́	about love
не на́до	don't
изве́стный	well-known
кинокри́тик	cinema critic
челове́к	person
ча́сто	often
Дом кино́	a well-known Moscow art house and cinema
же	but (adds emphasis)
вме́сте	together
Во́лга	Volga river
дово́льно	rather
индустриа́льный	industrial
го́род	town
везде́	everywhere
вку́сный	tasty
куда́	where to
Пойдёмте!	Let's go!
счёт	bill
Ого́!	Aha! (exclamation)
инфля́ция	inflation
три́ста	three hundred
рубль (m.)	rouble
рубле́й	of roubles
холо́дный	cold
окро́шка	okroshka (cold soup made from kvas or kefir and chopped meats and / or vegetables)
всегда́	always

Во́лга

The largest and longest European river, the Volga, is 3600 kilometres long. It's source is north of Moscow, and it flows through Central Russia to the Caspian Sea. The Volga is joined up to Moscow and Saint Petersburg by canals, lakes, and other rivers, and is one of Western Russia's major transport links.

Ключ

1 Яросла́вль
2 Ни́жний Но́вгород
3 Сара́нск
4 Каза́нь
5 Тамбо́в
6 Воро́неж
7 Сама́ра
8 Сара́тов
9 Волгогра́д
10 Астрахань

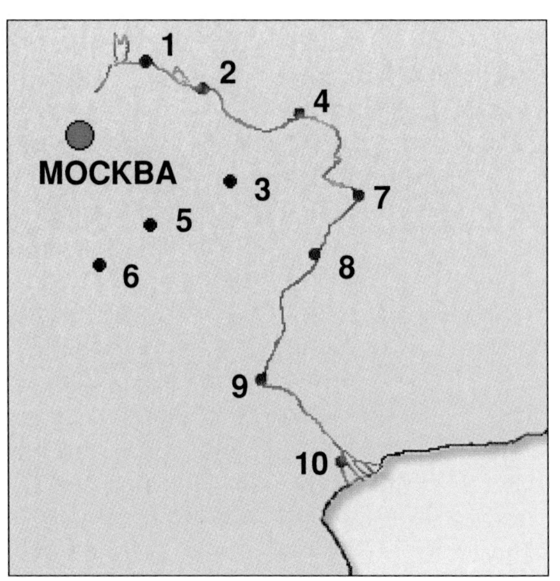

Ка́рта Во́лги

Pair work

- Сара́нск на Во́лге?
- Нет! Сара́нск не на Во́лге. А Сара́тов?
- Да. Сара́тов на Во́лге.

etc.

На Во́лге - перево́зка не́фти
On the Volga - transportation of oil

Verb review
Use the verb section in the grammar summary pages 134 and 135 to revise the verbs that you have met so far.

Что вы лю́бите де́лать? - What do you like doing?
For this construction use люби́ть plus the infinitive.

Я люблю́ чита́ть. I love reading (I love to read).

Neuter forms of verbs in the present tense are the same as the masculine or feminine forms:

Бюро́ рабо́тает. The office is working (open).
Вре́мя идёт. Time passes.

In the past tense the neuter ending is -ло

Это бы́ло интере́сно. That was interesting.

The preposition "о" means "about", and takes the prepositional case, which you met in lesson 4.

Вади́м - о Вади́ме
Москва́ - о Москве́
любо́вь - о любви́ (feminine soft sign nouns)
Росси́я - о Росси́и

Before vowels the letter б is inserted to separate the sounds:

о́пера - об о́пере
и́мя - об и́мени
"about me" is - обо мне

Nouns ending in a soft sign -ь
These can be either masculine or feminine, and you have to learn the gender when you learn the word. There are two general rules:

Abstract nouns ending in -ь are feminine: любо́вь - love
Months of the year ending in -ь are masculine: ию́нь - June

When these nouns change, the endings are soft:

	Masculine			Feminine		
Nominative	ию́нь	-	June	любо́вь	-	love
Accusative	ию́нь	-	June	любо́вь	-	love
Genitive	ию́ня	-	of June	любви́	-	of love
Prepositional	в ию́не	-	in June	о любви́	-	about love

вре́мя - time
A small number of Russian nouns end in -мя. These are all neuter.

вре́мя - time
и́мя - first name

The accusative is the same as the nominative: вре́мя / и́мя
The genitive and prepositional is вре́мени / и́мени.
The full declension of these nouns is given on page 133.

Impersonal constructions and adverbs

You can often form these from adjectives:

интере́сный челове́к	-	an interesting person
Это интере́сно.		That's interesting.
хоро́ший рестора́н	-	a good restaurant
Это хорошо́!		That's good!
Она́ хорошо́ рабо́тает.		She works well.

ЦИФРЫ NUMBERS

www

Numbers above 100

100	сто	1000	ты́сяча
101	сто оди́н	1100	ты́сяча сто
102	сто два	2000	две ты́сячи
150	сто пятьдеся́т	3000	три ты́сячи
200	две́сти	4000	четы́ре ты́сячи
300	три́ста	5000	пять ты́сяч
400	четы́реста	10000	де́сять ты́сяч
500	пятьсо́т	21000	два́дцать одна́ ты́сяча
600	шестьсо́т	22000	два́дцать две ты́сячи
700	семьсо́т	100.000	сто ты́сяч
800	восемьсо́т	1.000.000	миллио́н
900	девятьсо́т	1.000.000.000	миллиа́рд

The Russians use a full stop to separate thousands in the longer numbers.
They use a comma for the decimal point.

68

Buying 100 shashlyks - a dialogue for pronunciation practice

- Что вам ну́жно?
- Шашлыки́! Сто штук.
- Что?
- Шашлыки́!
- Ско́лько?
- Сто штук.
- Сто штук?
- Да, сто штук.
- Хорошо́!

"**Да́йте, пожа́луйста, два шашлыка́!**"

УПРАЖНЕНИЯ УРОК 7

1. Answer the questions on the text

а. Людми́ла ду́мает, что рестора́н хоро́ший?
б. Что Людми́ла лю́бит де́лать в свобо́дное вре́мя?
в. Ива́н чита́л кни́гу Вади́ма?
г. Го́род Сара́нск на Во́лге?
д. Го́род Сара́нск далеко́ от Во́лги?
е. Сара́нск - э́то индустриа́льный го́род?
ж. Ива́н хорошо́ зна́ет Вади́ма?

2. Fill in the gaps according to the text

а. Ива́н ________ и ________ в Сара́нске.
б. Людми́ла ________ ________ телеви́зор.
в. Вади́м ча́сто ________ Людми́лу в кино́.
г. Сара́нск _______ индустриа́льный ______.
д. Людми́ла __________ домо́й.

идёт
лю́бит
рабо́тает
большо́й
живёт
приглаша́ет
го́род
смотре́ть

3. Fill in the gaps to complete the dialogue

Что вы ________ в свобо́дное вре́мя?
Я люблю́ ________ кни́ги.
А вы лю́бите ________ в кино́?
Да, коне́чно ________.
А сего́дня вы ________ на о́перу?
Да, ________.
Кто вас ________?
__________!

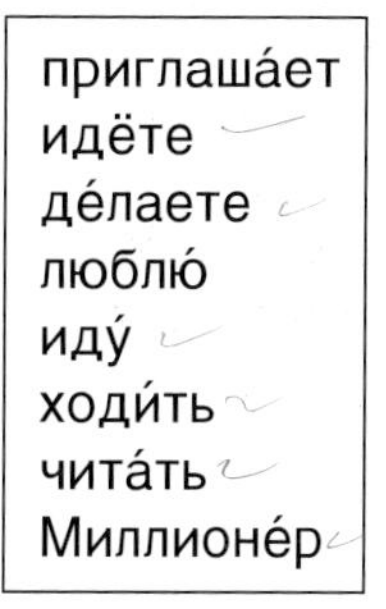
приглаша́ет
идёте
де́лаете
люблю́
иду́
ходи́ть
чита́ть
Миллионе́р

4. People like to talk about their own jobs or places of work! Make up sentences

Наприме́р: "Футболи́ст говори́т о футбо́ле."

стюарде́сса	компью́тер
актёр	ко́смос
почтальо́н	фильм
программи́ст	теа́тр
журнали́ст	по́чта
космона́вт	тра́ктор
музыка́нт	журна́л
кинокри́тик	аэропо́рт
шофёр	му́зыка
трактори́ст	такси́

1. **Which town is which?**

www

а. Большóй индустриáльный гóрод на Вóлге. В Совéтский периóд э́то был закры́тый гóрод. Метрó. Кремль. Аэропóрт. Речнóй вокзáл. ____________________

б. Этот гóрод пострóил Пётр Пéрвый на рекé Невé. Он был столи́цей Росси́и. Это бы́ло "окнó в Еврóпу". Там в 1917г. началáсь Октя́брьская революция. Эрмитáж. Зи́мний Дворéц. Метрó. Аэропóрт. ____________________

в. Большóй индустриáльный гóрод в Сиби́ри, недалекó от óзера Байкáл. Метрó. Аэропóрт. ____________________

г. Столи́ца Росси́и. Полити́ческий и культу́рный центр страны́. Четы́ре аэропóрта. Метрó. Кремль. ____________________

Ирку́тск
Москвá
Санкт-Петербу́рг
Ни́жний Нóвгород

2. **А где вы живёте?**
With the help of your teacher write a few phrases about your own neighbourhood or town.

____
____
____
____
____
____
____
____

Listen to the conversation between Вади́м and Ве́ра 69

1. Where had Ве́ра seen Людми́ла and Ива́н?
2. What did Вади́м think was funny?
3. Is Ве́ра interested in Ива́н?
4. Is Вади́м eager to introduce Ве́ра to Ива́н?

Ни́жний Но́вгород - у́лица Больша́я Покро́вка

ГОВОРИТЕ!

1. **Verb practice**

   Make cards for some of the infinitives you know. Write each infinitive on a separate card. Make a second set of cards for the personal pronouns: я, ты, он, она́, мы, вы, они́.

   One person turns up a verb card, another turns up a pronoun card. Then say the pronoun with the verb and the correct ending as quickly as you can.

   "Я люблю́!"

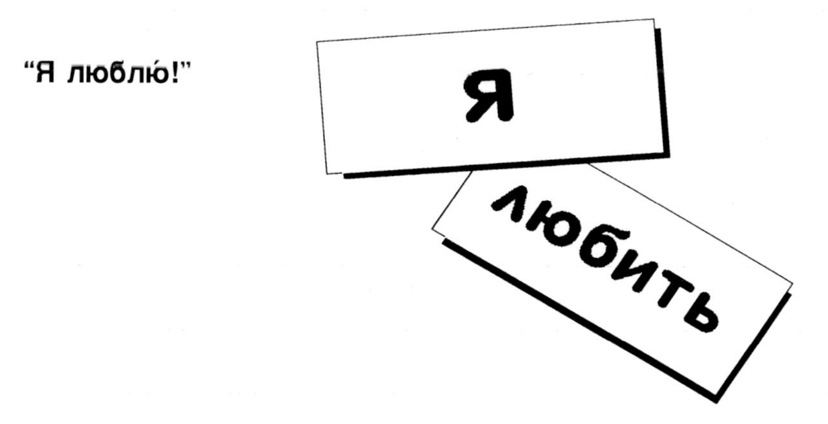

2. Ask each other questions in pairs

- Вы лю́бите чита́ть кни́ги?
- Вы лю́бите смотре́ть телеви́зор?
- Вы лю́бите ходи́ть в рестора́н?
- Вы лю́бите слу́шать му́зыку?
- Вы лю́бите ходи́ть в теа́тр?

Find others in the group who share your likes and dislikes

- Вы лю́бите чита́ть кни́ги?
- Да. Люблю́.
- Я то́же. А вы лю́бите смотре́ть телеви́зор?
- Да, о́чень.
- А я нет!

3. Communicative activity for a group

Decide three places you are going to from the list. Then try to find someone else in the group going to any of the same places.

парк - банк - стадио́н - рестора́н - аэропо́рт - гости́ница поликли́ника - университе́т - кинотеа́тр - магази́н

Пи́тер: Вы идёте в парк?
Ни́на: Нет. Я иду́ в поликли́нику, в банк и в рестора́н. А куда́ вы идёте?
Пи́тер: Я иду́ в парк, в гости́ницу и в рестора́н.
Ни́на: Хорошо́. Пойдёмте вме́сте в рестора́н.
Пи́тер: Очень хорошо́!

4. Game in a circle

Stand in a circle of up to six people.
One person says where he or she is going:
Пи́тер: Я иду́ в рестора́н.

The next person in the circle repeats this in the third person and adds his or her own statement:
Ни́на: Пи́тер идёт в рестора́н, а я иду́ в буфе́т.

The next person adds on another item, making the sentence longer all the time, until you have been round the whole ring.

Then everyone talks to everyone else, trying to remember where they are going:

- Вы идёте в центр, да?
- Да, а вы идёте в банк?
- Нет, я иду́ в поликли́нику.

LESSON 8	ВРЕМЯ	УРОК 8

Peter arrives in Moscow and makes contact with Vadim and Lyudmila. Ivan invites Lyudmila out to the opera.

You will meet the following grammatical points:
- ❑ the nominative plural of nouns and adjectives.
- ❑ the genitive plural of masculine nouns.
- ❑ the short adjective ну́жен - "necessary".
- ❑ short adjectives in the plural.
- ❑ the irregular verb мочь - "to be able to".

There is information about using the telephone in Russia.

By the end of the lesson you should be able to:
- ❑ tell the time in whole hours.
- ❑ understand the time zones in Russia.
- ❑ make simple phone calls and answer the telephone.

The **Ruslan 1 Workbook** contains 20 additional exercises for this lesson, including 4 listening exercises.
In the **Ruslan 1 Reader**, Igor is looking for a cash machine in Novosibirsk.
The **Ruslan 1 CD Rom** contains 33 additional exercises with sound, and including a video exercise.

Ру́сский анекдо́т

- У вас така́я хоро́шая жена́. Она́ всё вре́мя на ку́хне.
- Да, но э́то потому́, что у нас на ку́хне телефо́н!

всё вре́мя - all the time
на ку́хне - in the kitchen

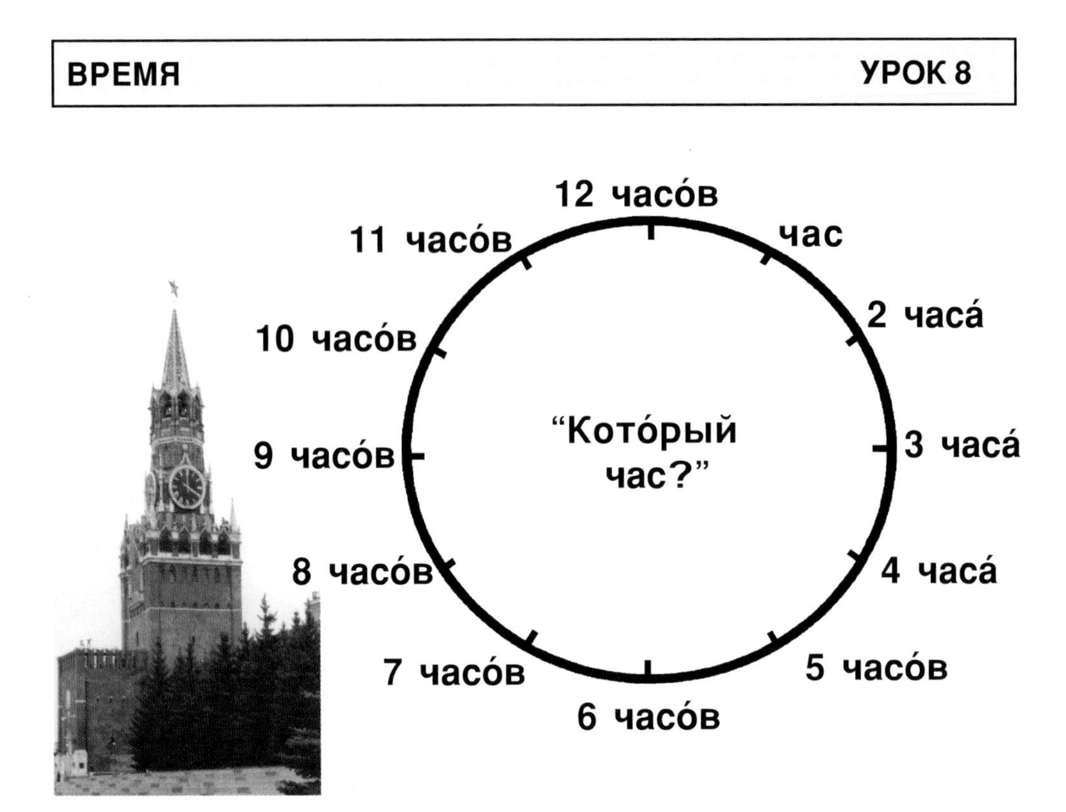

There are two ways of asking the time: "Кото́рый час?" and "Ско́лько вре́мени?"

One o'clock is just	Час	
Two o'clock	Два часа́	these take
Three o'clock	Три часа́	the genitive
Four o'clock	Четы́ре часа́	singular
Five o'clock	Пять часо́в	numerals
Six o'clock	Шесть часо́в	from 5 to 20
etc.		take the
Twelve o'clock	Двена́дцать часо́в	genitive plural

The 24-hour clock is used frequently, especially for official notoces, timetables etc.

14.00	Четы́рнадцать часо́в
21.00	Два́дцать оди́н час
22.30	Два́дцать два три́дцать
etc.	

В кото́ром часу́? - At what time?

To ask "At what time?", say: "Во ско́лько?" or "В кото́ром часу́?". The latter is more formal.

To reply "At seven o'clock", say: "В семь часо́в".

5:00

Peter arrived last night and wakes up in his hotel, already talking to himself in Russian!

71/74

Пи́тер: Где я? Кото́рый час? Уже́ де́сять часо́в! Хорошо́. А где здесь телефо́н?

He dials the number

Вади́м: Алло́!
Пи́тер: Вади́м Бори́сович? До́брое у́тро! Это Пи́тер говори́т. Пи́тер из Ло́ндона. Вы меня́ по́мните?
Вади́м: Пи́тер! Ну, коне́чно, по́мню! Вы в Москве́? Когда́ вы прие́хали?
Пи́тер: Вчера́ ве́чером.
Вади́м: Каки́е у вас пла́ны?
Пи́тер: У меня́ ма́ло вре́мени, но сего́дня я свобо́ден.
Вади́м: Тогда́, приезжа́йте к нам. Где вы сейча́с?
Пи́тер: В гости́нице “Марс”.
Вади́м: Это совсе́м бли́зко. Я о́чень рад. Вы звони́те из гости́ницы?
Пи́тер: Да, из гости́ницы. Запиши́те мой но́мер телефо́на: 241-05-79.
Вади́м: Приезжа́йте сего́дня ве́чером!
Пи́тер: Отли́чно! А когда́?
Вади́м: В семь часо́в.
Пи́тер: Очень хорошо́. Спаси́бо.
Вади́м: Хорошо́, мы все вас ждём в семь часо́в ве́чера.
Пи́тер: А кто все?
Вади́м: Я, ма́ма и Людми́ла. Вы по́мните Людми́лу?
Пи́тер: Ну, коне́чно, по́мню! Я о́чень рад! Слу́шайте, Вади́м Бори́сович, мне нужны́ ру́сские де́ньги. У меня́ нет де́нег... Алло́! Алло́! Что э́то? Телефо́н не рабо́тает ...

The part of Peter is played by Brian Savin, who learned Russian at evening classes. Brian's pronunciation is good for a learner, although he does have a slight English accent. (ed.)

72/75

The same day in the evening. The telephone rings again

Вади́м: Я слу́шаю.
Ива́н: Людми́лу Григо́риевну, пожа́луйста.
Вади́м: Кто говори́т?
Ива́н: Ива́н Козло́в.
Вади́м: Ах, вот как! Сейча́с... Лю́да, вас спра́шивают!

Lyudmila comes to the phone

73/76

Людми́ла:	Алло́! Я слу́шаю. До́брый ве́чер.
Ива́н:	Людми́ла! Говори́т Ива́н. Как у вас дела́?
Людми́ла:	Ничего́, спаси́бо. А у вас?
Ива́н:	Людми́ла, я приглаша́ю вас на о́перу в Большо́й теа́тр.
Людми́ла:	Когда́?
Ива́н:	Сего́дня ве́чером.
Людми́ла:	Сего́дня я не могу́.
Ива́н:	Тогда́ за́втра в семь часо́в. Вы свобо́дны за́втра?
Людми́ла:	За́втра? Пока́, да. Но приеха́л Пи́тер из Ло́ндона, и я не зна́ю, каки́е у него́ пла́ны. А биле́ты уже́ есть?
Ива́н:	Нет, биле́тов нет, но мо́жно заказа́ть в гости́нице.
Людми́ла:	Тогда́ закажи́те, пожа́луйста. А где мы встре́тимся?
Ива́н:	Встре́тимся в гости́нице в шесть часо́в. Хорошо́?
Людми́ла:	Хорошо́. До за́втра.

Кото́рый час?	What is the time?
у́тро	morning
До́брое у́тро!	Good morning!
по́мнить	to remember
прие́хать (perf.)	to arrive
ве́чер	evening
ве́чером	in the evening
ма́ло	little, not much
ноль (m.)	zero
Приезжа́йте!	Come! (by transport)
к нам	to our place
совсе́м	quite
звони́ть	to ring
записа́ть (perf.)	to write down
отли́чно	excellent
все	everybody
мне	for me
ну́жен / -на́ / -но / -ны́	necessary
Мне нужны́	I need (plural)
де́ньги (plural)	money
Вот как!	So that's the way it is!
До́брый ве́чер!	Good evening!
Как дела́?	How are things?
ничего́	alright (the "г" is pronounced "v")
мочь	to be able to
пока́	for now, for the moment
у него́	he has (the "г" is pronounced "v")
мы встре́тимся	we will meet

ИНФОРМАЦИЯ УРОК 8

Телефо́н

Public phones - Таксофо́ны - take phone cards in the more Westernised cities, and elsewhere tokens. You can buy these from kiosks or in the метро́.

Russians can be quite abrupt on the telephone, and this can make talking on the phone difficult, even for confident speakers of the language.

Таксофо́ны

When the phone is first answered you are often not told who is speaking. You will just hear "Алло́!" or "Да!".

When Russians read out a phone number they usually combine the first three numbers into one, and then the next four numbers in two pairs:

230 16 72

Две́сти три́дцать. Шестна́дцать. Се́мьдесят два.

It may be easier for you to read out single digits only:

Два, три, ноль. Оди́н, шесть. Семь, два.

ГРАММАТИКА УРОК 8

The nominative plural of nouns

Most masculine nouns add -ы or -и to the end of the word, depending on the spelling rule below, or -и replaces -й or -ь.
Feminine nouns replace -а with -ы or -и, -ь with -и and -ия with -ии.
Neuter nouns change -о to -а, -е to -я, -ие to -ия and -мя to -мена́.

Spelling rule
ы cannot follow: г, ж, к, х, ч, ш, or щ. It is replaced by и.
This is why the nominative plural of кни́га is кни́ги.

There are often stress changes.

Singular	Plural	Singular	Plural
план	пла́ны	трамва́й	трамва́и
у́лица	у́лицы	у́тро	у́тра
кни́га	кни́ги	мо́ре	моря́
река́	ре́ки	зда́ние	зда́ния
рубль	рубли́	и́мя	имена́
Several masculine nouns use a stressed -á			
па́спорт	паспорта́	дом	дома́
го́род	города́	а́дрес	адреса́
Certain masculine nouns lose a "fleeting" -о- or -е- :			
оте́ц	отцы́	переу́лок	переу́лки

The accusative plural of masculine and feminine inanimate nouns and of all neuter nouns is the same as the nominative plural.

Я зна́ю ва́ши пла́ны. I know your plans.

де́ньги - money

Several words, including де́ньги - "money" - exist in the plural only.

The plural of adjectives

Adjectives end in -ые or -ие in the nominative and accusative plural:

каки́е пла́ны?	what plans?	больши́е авто́бусы	large buses
но́вые кни́ги	new books	краси́вые города́	beautiful towns
ру́сские имена́	Russian names		

The genitive plural of masculine nouns

For most masculine nouns that end in a consonant, add -ов.

биле́т	нет биле́тов
авто́бус	мно́го авто́бусов
час	пять часо́в

Other masculine forms and feminine and neuter forms are in lesson 10 and in the grammar review.

Use the genitive plural after words like мно́го - "many", after нет with nouns in the plural, to translate "of" with nouns in the plural, after certain prepositions with nouns in the plural, and after numerals five and above.

мно́го домо́в	гру́ппа тури́стов	девятна́дцать студе́нтов
нет тарака́нов	пять часо́в	два́дцать шесть киломе́тров
далеко́ от городо́в		

Вас спра́шивают. Someone is asking for you.

The third person plural without они́ is used to mean "someone".

Вас приглаша́ют на конце́рт. You are invited to a concert.

The short adjective ну́жен - necessary

In the masculine this has a fleeting -е-, which it loses in the other genders. Also there are stress changes.

Он не ну́жен.	He isn't needed.
Деклара́ция не нужна́.	The declaration isn't necessary.
Такси́ ну́жно?	Do you need a taxi?

Short adjectives in the plural

These add -ы to the stem (or sometimes -и, see the spelling rule page 98.)

Мне нужны́ ру́сские де́ньги.	I need some Russian money
Ба́нки бы́ли закры́ты.	The banks were shut.

мочь - to be able to - an irregular verb

я могу́, ты мо́жешь, он / она́ мо́жет, мы мо́жем, вы мо́жете, они́ мо́гут

Я не зна́ю, каки́е у него́ пла́ны. I don't know what plans he has.

In lesson 5 you met у меня́ and у вас used for "I have" and "you have". Similarly:

у него́	-	he has	у неё -	she has
у них	-	they have		

1. Да и́ли нет?

а. Вади́м по́мнит Пи́тера.
б. У Пи́тера мно́го вре́мени.
в. Вади́м рад, что Пи́тер в гости́нице "Марс".
г. Пи́тер по́мнит Людми́лу.
д. Ива́н приглаша́ет Людми́лу на о́перу.
е. У Ива́на есть биле́ты.
ж. У Людми́лы есть биле́ты.
з. Биле́ты мо́жно заказа́ть в гости́нице.
и. Людми́ла зна́ет, каки́е пла́ны у Пи́тера.

2. Fill in the gaps in the phone conversation

- Алло́
- Кто ___________?
- Это Пи́тер. Вы меня́ ___________ ?
- Коне́чно, ___________. Каки́е у вас ___________ на сего́дня?
- У меня́ нет ___________.
- Пожа́луйста, приезжа́йте __________.
- С удово́льствием. А ___________ ?
- Приезжа́йте в во́семь ___________.
- __________ хорошо́!

по́мню
Очень
говори́т
пла́нов
пла́ны
часо́в
по́мните
когда́
к нам

3. Rewrite these sentences in the plural

а. Тури́ст чита́ет журна́л.
б. Тури́стка чита́ет кни́гу.
в. Инжене́р был здесь.
г. Но́вый студе́нт то́же был здесь.
д. Магази́н откры́т.
е. Это но́вый телеви́зор?
ж. Англи́йский бизнесме́н не говори́т по-ру́сски.

4. Rewrite these sentences in the singular

а. Кинокри́тики обе́дают.
б. Это ру́сские города́.
в. Рестора́ны откры́ты.
г. Это хоро́шие биле́ты.

5. Fill in the gaps. Change the endings as necessary

В Москве́ мно́го _________, _________, _________, и _________.

В Москве́ ма́ло _________.

авто́бусы - теа́тры - кана́лы - па́рки - тури́сты

1. Peter is a teacher of Russian literature and wants to visit the graves of several Russian authors while he is in Moscow. They are: Anton Chekhov, Sergei Esenin, Nikolai Gogol', Vladimir Mayakovsky, Bulat Okudzhava and Nikolai Ostrovsky.

   Here is a list of where literary figures are buried in Moscow. Make a note of which cemetery he will find each of the graves in.

Никола́й Васи́льевич Го́голь

КЛАДБИЩА, ГДЕ ПОХОРОНЕНЫ ЛИТЕРАТОРЫ

Армянское кладбище. ул. Сергея Макеева, 12.
Здесь похоронен А.П.Платонов.

Ваганьковское кладбище. ул. Сергея Макеева, 15.
Похоронены: А.К.Виноградов, В.С.Высоцкий, С.А.Есенин, В.И.Даль, А.С.Неверов, Б.Ш.Окуджава, Ю.Н.Тынянов, Ф.С.Шкулев.

Введенское кладбище. Наличная ул.,1.
Похоронены: Д.В.Кедрин, С.Г.Скиталец, Л.Н.Сейфуллина.

Донской монастырь. Донская площадь,1.
На кладбище монастыря похоронены: И.И.Дмитриев, И.М.Долгорукий, В.И.Майков, В.Ф.Одоевский, А.П.Сумароков, М.М.Херасков, П.Я.Чаадаев.

Новодевичье кладбище. ул. Хамовнический Вал, 50.
Похоронены: С.Т.Аксаков, Э.Г.Багрицкий, Демьян Бедный, Андрей Белый, В.Я.Брюсов, М.А.Булгаков, В.В.Вересаев, Н.В.Гоголь, Д.В.Давыдов, И.А.Ильф, С.Я.Маршак, В.В.Маяковский, А.Н.Островский, А.Т.Твардовский, А.Н.Толстой, А.А.Фадеев, Д.А.Фурманов, А.П.Чехов, В.М.Шукшин, И.Г.Эренбург.

кла́дбище	a cemetery
кла́дбища	cemeteries
похоро́нен	is buried
похоро́нены	are buried
литера́тор	literary figure

For an exercise on Russian names, linked to this page, please go to: www.ruslan.co.uk/ruslan1.htm

2. What is on sale at the Маркон trading hall, and where do the goods come from?

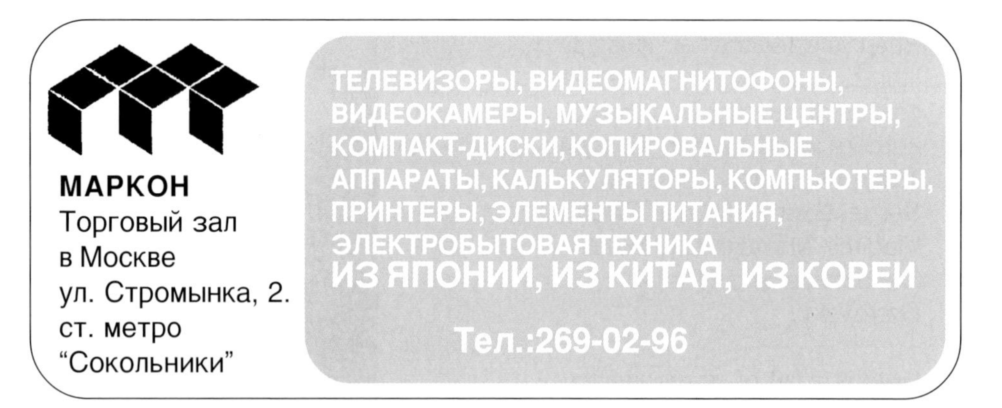

СЛУШАЙТЕ!

77 **Ivan is trying to book theatre tickets:**

1. Which theatre is he trying to get the tickets for?
2. When does he want to go to the theatre?
3. He was offered two possibilities, the ballet "Щелку́нчик" (The Nutcracker) and the opera "Снегу́рочка". Which did he choose and why?
4. What time does the evening performance start?

ГОВОРИТЕ!

1. **Role-play. You have just arrived in Moscow and you telephone a friend (another student or your teacher):**

Say "hello".	Ask who is there.
Say who you are and where you are from. Ask if he / she remembers you.	Yes, of course you remember him / her. Ask if he / she has any plans.
Say you have no plans.	Ask where he / she is.
In the hotel "Sputnik".	Ask for the phone number.
212 45 26.	Ask if he / she can come this evening.
Say yes, very good. Ask at what time you should come.	Suggest at 6 o'clock.
Say that's excellent.	End the conversation.

Россия́ - ка́рта часовы́х поясо́в - a map of the time zones

2. Work in pairs, asking each other questions

- В Москве́ два часа́. Кото́рый час в Новосиби́рске?
- В Новосиби́рске пять часо́в.

- В Бра́тске шесть часо́в. Кото́рый час в Москве́?
- В Москве́ час.

First use the map, then try to remember without it.

3. In a group, each learner is in a different town. Decide which.
Then one person says what time it is in his or her town and others have to say what time it is in theirs.

Арха́нгельск - Братск - Верхоя́нск - Волгогра́д
Владивосто́к - Екатеринбу́рг - Ирку́тск - Магада́н
Москва́ - Му́рманск - Новосиби́рск - Омск
Сама́ра - Санкт-Петербу́рг - Томск - Яку́тск

Ivan and Lyudmila are at the opera. Lyudmila doesn't like the seats, but she does enjoy the performance.

In the interval Lyudmila telephones Zoya Petrovna to find out what Peter is doing. Then Ivan invites her to the Botanical Gardens.

You will meet the following grammatical points:
- ❑ reflexive verbs in the present tense, for example начина́ться - "to begin".
- ❑ the dative singular of nouns.
- ❑ the difference between the transitive verb люби́ть - "to love", and the intransitive verb нра́виться - "to please", which is used to convey "to like".
- ❑ the use of раз - "a time".

There is information about the tale of "Snegurochka".

By the end of the lesson you should be able to:
- ❑ talk about your likes and dislikes.
- ❑ understand a theatre programme.
- ❑ talk about which sports you play or used to play.

> The **Ruslan 1 Workbook** contains 17 additional exercises for this lesson, including 3 listening exercises.
> In the **Ruslan 1 Reader**, Igor and Nellie go to the theatre, and there is a song for learners: "Конце́рт".
> The **Ruslan 1 CDRom** contains 30 additional exercises with sound.

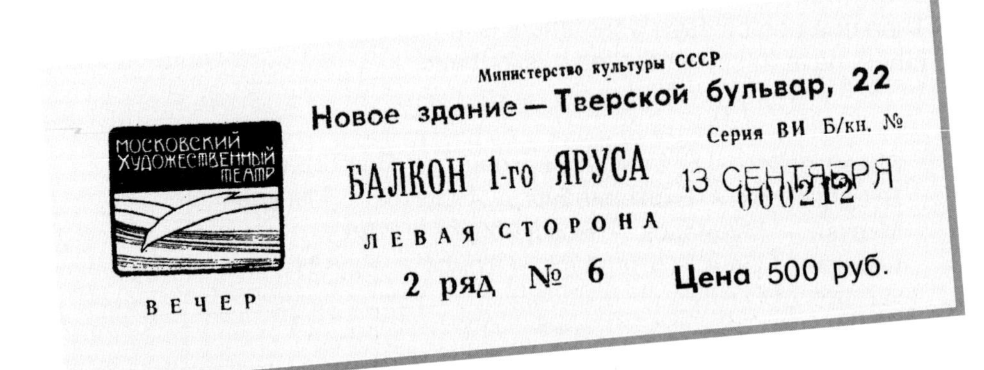

79/84

В теа́тре

Людми́ла: Скоре́е, о́пера уже́ начина́ется. Где на́ши места́?
Ива́н: На балко́не.
Людми́ла: На балко́не? Каки́е плохи́е места́!
Ива́н: Ну, что тепе́рь де́лать!?

80/85

В антра́кте

Ива́н: Вам нра́вится о́пера?
Людми́ла: Да, о́чень нра́вится. А кто игра́ет роль Снегу́рочки? Мо́жно посмотре́ть програ́ммку?
Ива́н: Вот, пожа́луйста. А вы не хоти́те в буфе́т?
Людми́ла: Да, хочу́. Пойдёмте?

81/86

В буфе́те

Ива́н: Так вы уже́ ви́дели "Снегу́рочку" ра́ньше?
Людми́ла: Коне́чно, два и́ли три ра́за.
Ива́н: Что вы хоти́те - чай, ко́фе? Мо́жет быть, хоти́те вино́?
Людми́ла: Да, я хочу́ кра́сное вино́.
Ива́н: Да́йте, пожа́луйста, мне чай, а де́вушке вино́.
Людми́ла: Ива́н, здесь есть телефо́н?
Ива́н: Не зна́ю. А кому́ вы хоти́те позвони́ть? Вади́му?
Людми́ла: Нет. Мне на́до позвони́ть Зо́е Петро́вне.
Ива́н: Хорошо́. Я ду́маю, что телефо́н нале́во по коридо́ру. То́лько скоре́е. Второ́й акт начина́ется.

82/87

Людми́ла звони́т по телефо́ну

Людми́ла: Зо́я Петро́вна? Это Людми́ла. Да, я сейча́с в теа́тре. Да, мне о́чень нра́вится. Прекра́сная о́пера. И Ната́лья Ивано́ва прекра́сно игра́ет роль Снегу́рочки. Когда́ конча́ется? По́здно. Ду́маю, в де́сять часо́в. Не на́до ждать. А когда́ Пи́тер возвраща́ется? Он уже́ там? Что он де́лает? Игра́ет в ша́хматы? Молоде́ц! Скажи́те Вади́му, что за́втра я иду́ к врачу́. Хорошо́. Спаси́бо, до свида́ния.

83/88

Второ́й акт начина́ется

Ива́н: Ну как? Всё в поря́дке?
Людми́ла: Да. Всё в поря́дке. Спаси́бо.
Ива́н: Людми́ла, за́втра вы свобо́дны? Я приглаша́ю вас в Ботани́ческий сад. Там о́чень романти́чно ...
Людми́ла: Нет, спаси́бо. Я иду́ к подру́ге на день рожде́ния. Пойдёмте! Второ́й акт начина́ется ...

начина́ться	to begin
наш / на́ша / на́ше / на́ши	our
ме́сто	seat
места́	seats
балко́н	balcony
плохо́й	bad
антра́кт	interval
нра́виться	to please
игра́ть	to play
роль (f.)	role
програ́ммка	theatre programme
ви́деть	to see
ра́ньше	before
раз	time, occasion
на́до	it is necessary
позвони́ть (perf.)	to telephone
по (+ dat.)	along
коридо́р	corridor
второ́й	second
акт	act
конча́ться	to finish
возвраща́ться	to return
ша́хматы	chess
Молоде́ц!	Good lad! / Well done!
к (+ dat.)	to, towards
врач	doctor
поря́док	order
всё в поря́дке	everything is OK
ботани́ческий	botanical
сад	garden
романти́чно	romantic
подру́га	girl friend
день рожде́ния	birthday

"Молоде́ц!" can be used for males or females. It should not be used for one's superiors!

ИНФОРМАЦИЯ

Опера 'Снегу́рочка'

From the word снег - "snow", Снегу́рочка is a character from an old Russian fairy tale. A childless couple make a girl out of snow and adopt her. She is a charming girl, loved by everyone. When the summer comes she goes for a walk with her friends in the forest and melts away in the heat of the sun. The Russian writer A. Ostrovsky used the folk tale for his play of the same name, and it was later used by Rimsky-Korsakov for his opera. At the New Year, Снегу́рочка and her grandfather, Дед Моро́з - Grandfather Frost - visit Russian children with presents.

Снег и моро́з

Reflexive verbs have the ending -ся or -сь after a vowel

начина́ться - to begin   конча́ться - to finish   возвраща́ться - to return

я возвраща́юсь, ты возвраща́ешься, он / она́ возвраща́ется,
мы возвраща́емся, вы возвраща́етесь, они́ возвраща́ются

The dative singular of nouns

The dative is used to express the indirect object, for example:

Да́йте мне биле́т.	Give (to) me the ticket.
Я хочу́ позвони́ть Пи́теру.	I want to telephone (to) Peter.

Masculine and most neuter nouns have the endings -у or -ю.
Neuter nouns in -мя change to -мени and in -ие to -ию.
Feminine nouns change -а or -я to -е, -ь to -и, and -ия to -ии.
The dative of кто is кому́, of я is мне and of вы is вам.
The dative of он is ему́, of она́ is ей and of они́ is им.

See the tables on pages 132 and 133.

The dative is used after the prepositions по - "along" and к - "towards" or "to the place of":

Он идёт по коридо́ру.	He is walking along the corridor.
Я иду́ к подру́ге.	I am going to my girl friend's.

The dative is used in certain indirect expressions:

Вам нра́вится о́пера?	Do you like the opera? (Is it pleasing to you?)
Мне на́до рабо́тать.	I need to work. (For me it is necessary to work)
Пи́теру нужны́ де́ньги.	Peter needs money.
Студе́нтке пло́хо.	The female student is not well.

люби́ть / нра́виться

люби́ть is a transitive verb meaning "to love" or "to like very much".
It is followed by a direct object in the accusative.

Я люблю́ шокола́д.	I love chocolate.
Она́ лю́бит му́зыку.	She loves music.

нра́виться means "to please". It is used intransitively to render "to like".
What is liked is the subject of the sentence, and the person is in the dative.

Мне нра́вится пье́са.	I like the play. (The play is pleasing to me)
Она́ вам нра́вится?	Do you like her?

ви́деть - to see

я ви́жу, ты ви́дишь, он / она́ ви́дит, мы ви́дим, вы ви́дите, они́ ви́дят
Note the mutation in the first person singular from -д to -ж.

игра́ть в ша́хматы - to play chess

With sports, игра́ть is used with в and the accusative case.

www **раз - a time**

оди́н раз	-	once	
не оди́н раз	-	more than once	
три ра́за	-	three times	
пять раз	-	five times	
Ско́лько раз?	-	How many times?	

When counting, start with "раз": раз, два, три, четы́ре, пять ...

1. Да и́ли нет?

а. Людми́ла ду́мает, что места́ хоро́шие.
б. Людми́ле на́до позвони́ть в Ло́ндон.
в. Телефо́н нале́во по коридо́ру.
г. Ива́н приглаша́ет Людми́лу на конце́рт.
д. Опера конча́ется по́здно.
е. Пи́тер игра́ет в ша́хматы.

2. Fill in the gaps to complete the dialogue

- Зо́я Петро́вна? __________ ве́чер!
- До́брый __________! Вы в __________?
- Да, я в теа́тре.
- А как __________ нра́вится о́пера?
- Мне о́чень __________. Прекра́сная о́пера.
- А когда́ __________ конча́ется?
- Она́ __________ по́здно.
  Не __________ меня́__________.

она́
ве́чер
До́брый
ждать
конча́ется
вам
нра́вится
теа́тре
на́до

3. Fill in the gaps, choosing the correct alternative according to the story, and adding the dative endings

Людми́ла говори́т __________, что за́втра она́ идёт к __________, но она́ говори́т __________, что она́ идёт к __________ .

врач
Ива́н
Зо́я Петро́вна
подру́га

4. Во что они́ игра́ют? What do they play? www

Андре́й Арша́вин
Па́вел Буре́
Га́рри Каспа́ров
Мари́я Шара́пова
Андре́й Шевче́нко
Михаил Южный

Па́вел Буре́

5. А кто игра́ет в насто́льный те́ннис?

Отве́т: Влади́мир Пу́тин игра́ет в насто́льный те́ннис.

www

ТЕАТР НА ТАГАНКЕ
21 июня 2008г. в 20 часов
КОТ В САПОГАХ
Пьеса-сказка в 2 частях
Перевод Л. Гинзбурга
Действующие лица:

Кот	В. Иванов
Стефан	С. Маковецкий
Король	М. Шапиро
Принцесса	Л. Корнева
Солдат	И. Лагутин
Волшебник	В. Русланов
Крестьянин	А. Котрелев
Его жена	А. Козлова
Дуб	Д. Воронин
Берёза	А. Потапова
Ведьма	Д. Пешкова
Музыка	Е. Федоров
Танцы	Н. Иванова

1. What is on at the Taganka theatre, when and what time?
2. What parts are the following actors playing:
   Igor Lagutin, Larissa Kornyeva, Victor Ivanov?
3. Looking at the names, you can tell for sure whether they are male or female actors, except for one. Which?
4. Write sentences based on the advertisement. An example has been done for you.

   Note the two alternative ways of writing the letter "т" - *т/т*
   (Here we have used the second).

   И. Лагутин играет роль солдата.

   ____

   ____

   ____

   ____

For an exercise on Russian names linked to this page, please go to:
www.ruslan.co.uk/ruslan1.htm

1. Спекта́кли

а. Where are these ballets taking place?
б. Which of the ballets is about a French general?
в. Which orchestra is playing?

2. Демонстра́ция

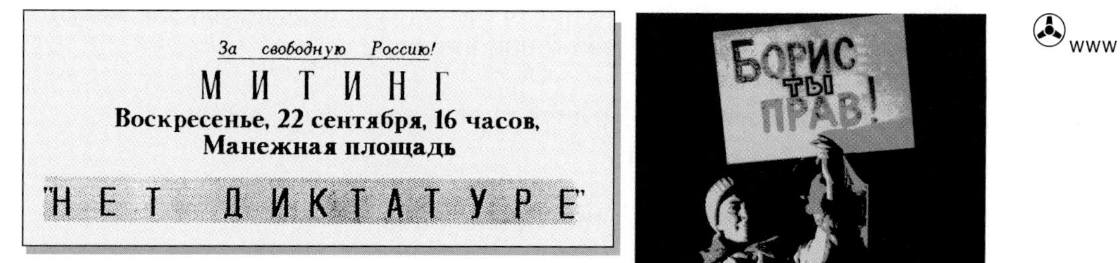

www

а. When and where is this demonstration taking place?
б. What is it called to say "no" to?
в. Does she support Boris or not?

СЛУШАЙТЕ!

Людми́ла is talking to her friend Тама́ра

89

1. When did Людми́ла go to see Тама́ра?
2. Does Тама́ра know that Ива́н is rich?
3. Has Тама́ра ever seen "Снегу́рочка"?
4. Is Людми́ла eager to introduce Ива́н to Тама́ра?

1. Role-play for pair work

Invite your partner to the Bolshoy theatre.	Ask what is on.
The play Hamlet. (Га́млет)	Say yes, with pleasure, but when?
Tomorrow evening.	At what time?
At 7 o'clock.	Very good.
Where shall we meet?	At the theatre.

2. Когда́ вы возвраща́етесь? When are you returning?

Imagine that the people in your group are going out for the day, coming back at different times. Each decide when you are coming back. One person then starts:

Питер: Я возвраща́юсь в 10 часо́в

The next person repeats this in the third person and adds his or her own time:

Ни́на: Питер возвраща́ется в 10 часо́в. Я возвраща́юсь в 9 часо́в.

And so on until you have been round the circle.

Then each student talks to everyone else, trying to remember when he / she is returning.

3. A guessing game using the dative case

You need a collection of real items or pictures:

па́спорт - кассе́та - вино́ - во́дка - лимона́д
биле́т - су́мка - де́ньги - газе́та - журна́л

and a list of professions:

журнали́ст - кинокри́тик - студе́нт - бизнесме́н
тракторист - программи́ст - врач - инжене́р - солда́т

One person goes out of the room. While he / she is out, let the others each choose a profession. Then ask him / her to come back.

Ask students to give instructions such as:

- Да́йте па́спорт журнали́сту!
- Да́йте су́мку студе́нту!

The person who has been out of the room has to use Russian to find out who is who and then give the items to the right people.

4. Вы игра́ете в те́ннис?

Find out what games or sports people play. Find out whether any people in the group play the same sports as you.

- Вы игра́ете в те́ннис?	- Нет.
- Вы игра́ете в футбо́л?	- Нет.
- Вы игра́ете в ша́хматы?	- Да.
- Я то́же игра́ю в ша́хматы.	- Хорошо́!
- Вы пла́ваете?	- Нет.

You can also talk about what sports you used to play in the past:
- Вы игра́ли в те́ннис?

Ви́ды спо́рта
бадминто́н
баскетбо́л
бейсбо́л
волейбо́л
гольф
дартс
крике́т
насто́льный те́ннис
ре́гби
те́ннис
футбо́л
хокке́й
ша́хматы

Премье́р-мини́стр игра́ет в футбо́л?

to swim	пла́вать
to run	бе́гать

5. Pair work - разгово́р по телефо́ну

Act out the telephone conversation between Lyudmila in the theatre and Zoya Petrovna, page 106, making up your own version of the part of Zoya Petrovna. First use the text in the book, then repeat the exercise from memory.

LESSON 10	ДОМ	УРОК 10

Lyudmila has a meal with her friend Tamara and talks about her trip to England. Tamara is interested in Lyudmila's male friends and would like to meet them. Lyudmila gets back to Zoya Petrovna's flat very late.

You will meet the following grammatical points:
- ❑ the instrumental singular of nouns.
- ❑ the spelling rule that affects the unstressed letter "o".
- ❑ the genitive plural of feminine nouns, of masculine and feminine. nouns that end in a soft sign, and of masculine nouns in -ж, ч, ш and щ.
- ❑ the declension of personal pronouns.
- ❑ the verbs спать - "to sleep" - and петь - "to sing".

The information section is about housing in Russia.

By the end of the lesson you should be able to:
- ❑ describe houses and flats in Russian.
- ❑ understand a Russian TV guide.
- ❑ talk about playing musical instruments.

The **Ruslan 1 Workbook** contains 23 additional exercises for this lesson, including 5 listening exercises.
In the **Ruslan 1 Reader** there is a text about Igor's visit to Nikolai and Nellie's dacha near Novosibirsk, and a poem for learners "Люблю́ на да́чу е́здить я!".
The **Ruslan 1 CDRom** contains 30 additional exercises with sound.

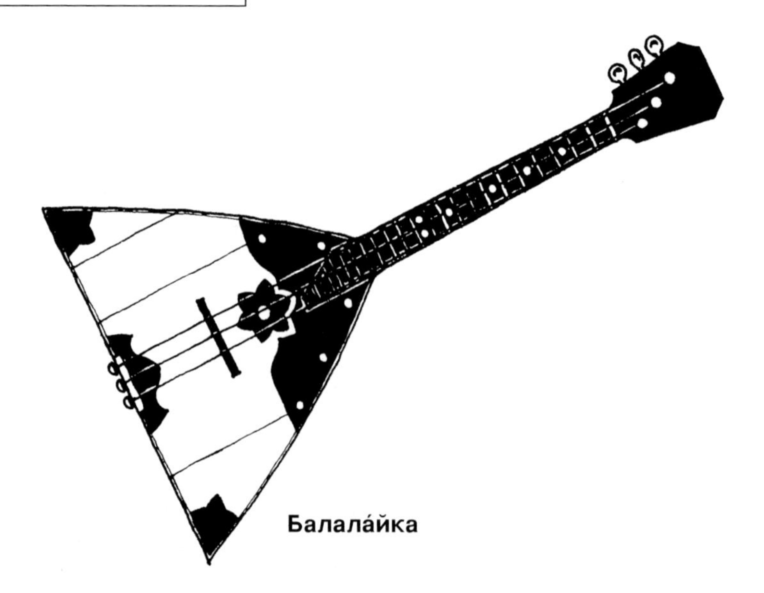

Балала́йка

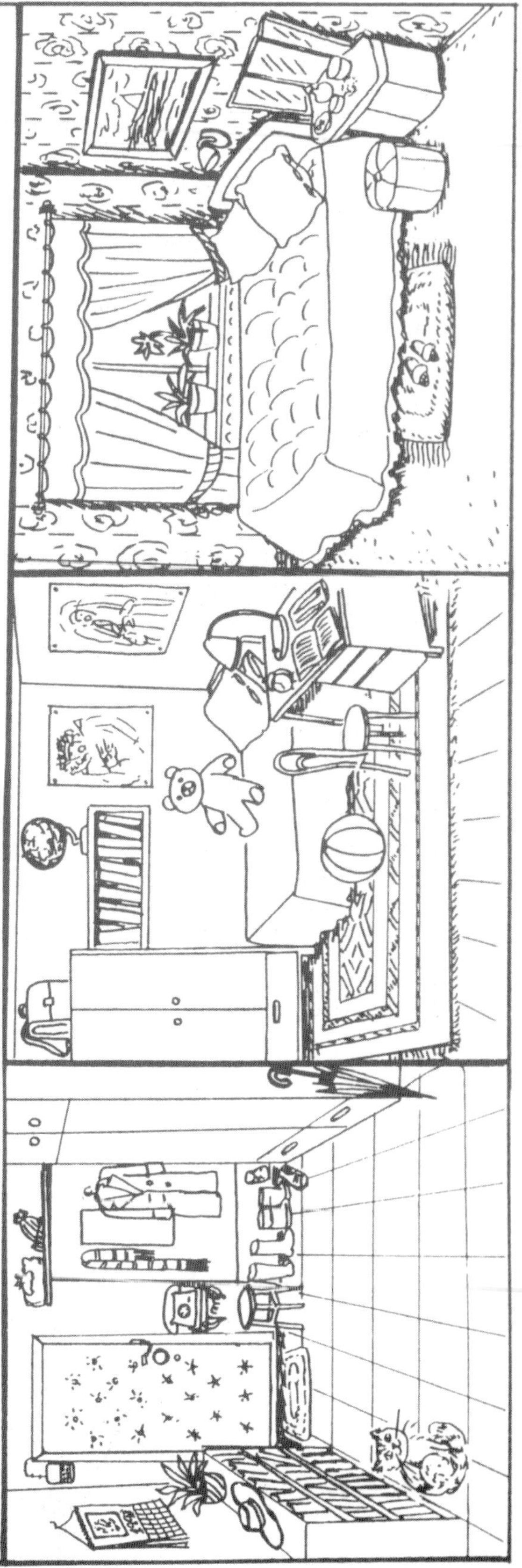

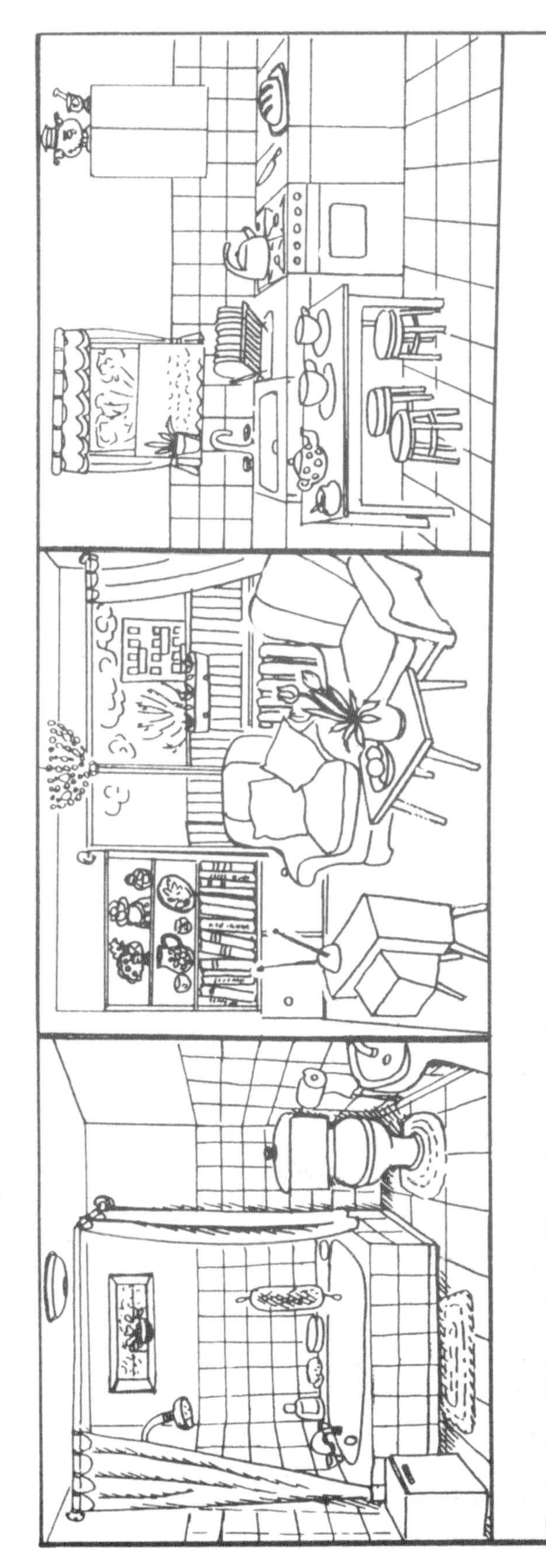

Lyudmila has just finished a meal at the flat of her friend Tamara

91
Людмила: Спасибо за обед. А уже поздно?
Тамара: Пять часов.
Людмила: Ну, мне пора.
Тамара: Нет, давай пить чай. С молоком или с лимоном?
Людмила: Ладно. С молоком, пожалуйста.

92
Тамара: Теперь расскажи о Лондоне. Сколько времени ты жила у Питера?
Людмила: Я была там пять дней.
Тамара: А Вадим знает?
Людмила: Конечно, нет. Я ничего не говорила Вадиму.

93
Тамара: Питер живёт в квартире?
Людмила: Нет. У него обычный английский дом.
Тамара: Как у тебя в Софрино?
Людмила: Нет, что ты! У него два этажа и все удобства - газ, электричество...
Тамара: Два этажа?! И балкон есть? А сколько комнат?
Людмила: Балкона нет, но есть гараж. Внизу - кухня, столовая и гостиная, а наверху - три спальни.
Тамара: А туалет, как в Софрино, на улице?
Людмила: У него два туалета - один внизу, другой наверху.
Тамара: А какая у него мебель?
Людмила: Мебель обычная - столы, стулья, книжные полки, много книг. Всё, как у меня в Софрино. Мне нравится его гостиная - большой удобный диван, два кресла и большой телевизор.

94
Тамара: Он часто смотрит телевизор?
Людмила: Нет. Он всё время работает с компьютером. Но он любит фильмы о Джеймсе Бонде. Мы смотрели фильм "Из России с любовью".
Тамара: Я думаю, что ему надо жениться. Он живёт один?
Людмила: Нет. Он живёт с мамой. Ты знаешь, сад у него очень красивый. Питер его очень любит и работает в нём каждый день. У него в саду очень много цветов, и в огороде много овощей.
Тамара: Сад! Это не интересно! Когда мне можно познакомиться с Питером?
Людмила: Я не знаю. Он очень занят. Он здесь по делу. А ты знаешь, он очень хорошо играет на гитаре и поёт.
Тамара: Хорошая ты подруга! У тебя есть миллионер из Саранска. Я его ещё не видела. Ну и, конечно, Вадим... он о тебе всё время говорит... А теперь этот англичанин!
Людмила: Ой, не надо! Мне пора идти!

At Zoya Petrovna's

95

Зо́я Петро́вна:	Людми́ла! Наконе́ц! Где вы бы́ли?
Людми́ла:	У подру́ги. Извини́те, что по́здно.
Зо́я Петро́вна:	А я сказа́ла Вади́му, что вы у врача́.
Людми́ла:	Да, я была́ у врача́ то́же. А где Пи́тер?
Зо́я Петро́вна:	Игра́ет в ша́хматы с Вади́мом.
Людми́ла:	Ла́дно. Я иду́ спать. Споко́йной но́чи!

Продолже́ние сле́дует - The story continues in Ruslan 2 and 3.

Спаси́бо за ...	Thank you for ...
Дава́й(те) ...!	Let's ...!
с (+ instr.)	with
ла́дно	fine, all right
ничего́	nothing
кварти́ра	flat
обы́чный	usual
эта́ж	floor
удо́бство	facility
газ	gas
электри́чество	electricity
внизу́	downstairs
ку́хня	kitchen
столо́вая	dining room
гости́ная	living room
наверху́	upstairs
спа́льня	bedroom
туале́т	toilet
на у́лице	outside
друго́й	another
ме́бель (f.)	furniture
обы́чный	ordinary, usual
стол	table
стул	chair
сту́лья	chairs
кни́жный	book (adj.)
по́лка	shelf
удо́бный	comfortable
дива́н	sofa
кре́сло	armchair
любо́вь (f.)	love
жени́ться	to get married (for a man)
сад	garden
цвето́к	a flower
цвето́в (gen. pl.)	of flowers
огоро́д	vegetable garden
о́вощи	vegetables
ка́ждый	every, each
де́ло	business
по де́лу	on business
гита́ра	guitar
петь	to sing
наконе́ц!	at last!
сказа́ть (perf.)	to tell
спать	to sleep
Споко́йной ночи!	Good night!

Со́фрино

This is a typical rural commuter settlement about 30 miles north of Moscow, outside the Moscow ring road. It has an interesting icon factory.

жени́ться - to get married

This is used for men and for couples. For women use "вы́йти за́муж" which literally means "to come out (of the church) after a man"!

Housing in Russia
In towns people live in large blocks of flats. In the Soviet Union, before the 1960s, there was a severe shortage of living space, but it is now the norm for each family to have its own flat.

In country areas people own small houses, often made of wood, and with some land attached.

Many town people own a **да́ча** - "summer house" - outside town, which they go to at weekends and for longer periods in the summer holiday. The **да́ча** is usually used for growing fruit and vegetables.

Recently **котте́джи** have started to appear, especially on the outskirts of large towns. These are not "cottages", but large new detached houses.

Кварти́ры в го́роде

Дом в дере́вне

www

For useful links for housing and furniture topics go to: www.ruslan.co.uk/ruslan1.htm

Но́вый котте́дж недалеко́ от Москвы́

Двухко́мнатная кварти́ра - a two-room flat
Там есть две ко́мнаты и ещё прихо́жая, ку́хня, ва́нная и туале́т.

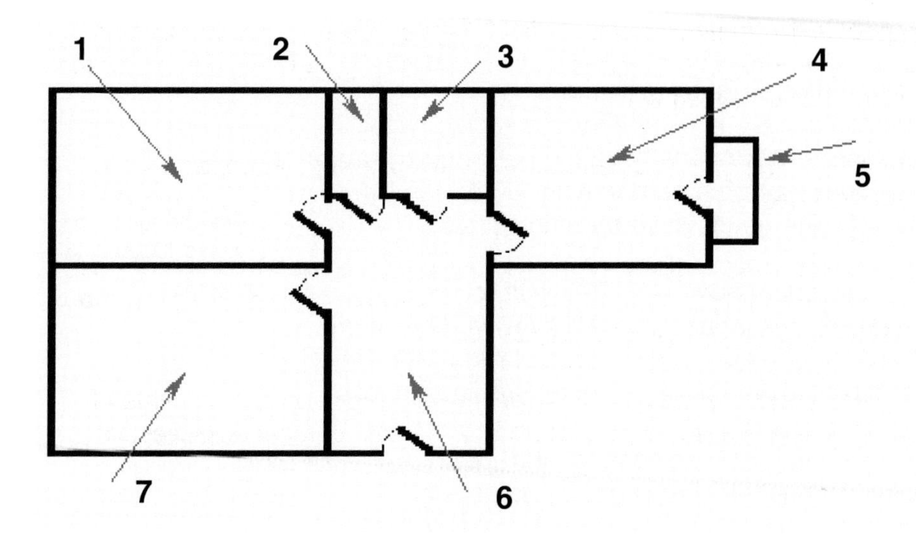

Ключ:

1. ку́хня
2. туале́т
3. ва́нная
4. спа́льня
5. балко́н
6. прихо́жая
7. гости́ная / спа́льня №2

Слова́рь:

ва́нная	-	bathroom
прихо́жая	-	hall
гости́ная	-	living room

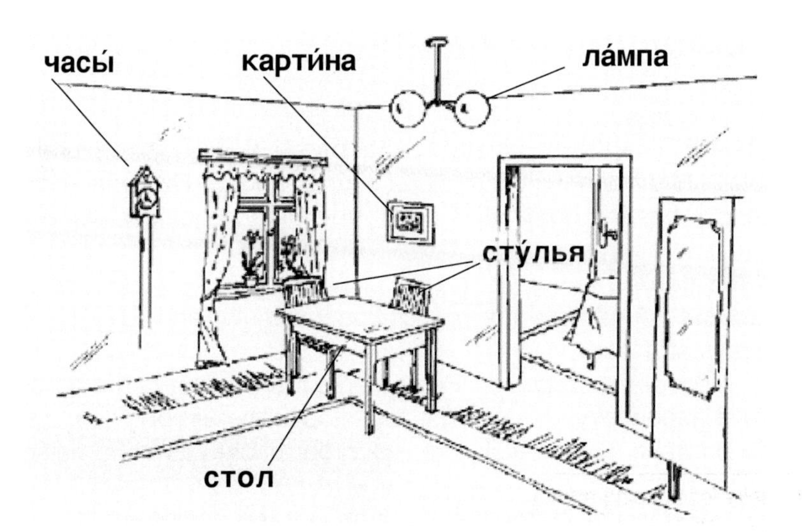

Спаси́бо за ... - Thank you for ... is used with the accusative case:

Спаси́бо за обе́д. Спаси́бо за кни́гу.

The instrumental singular of nouns

The instrumental case is used after с meaning "with".
Masculine and neuter nouns have the hard ending -ом or soft -ем.
Feminine nouns have the hard ending -ой or soft -ей.
Feminine soft sign nouns have the ending -ью.

See the tables on pages 132 and 133.

чай с лимо́ном -	tea with lemon
Он живёт с ма́мой.	He lives with his mum.
Я игра́ю с Ка́тей.	I am playing with Katya.
из Росси́и с любо́вью -	from Russia with love

мать - "mother" - changes to ма́терью
дочь - "daughter" - changes to до́черью

For other uses of the instrumental see Ruslan 2 and Ruslan 3.

Spelling rule for unstressed letter о

Unstressed о cannot follow ж, ц, ч, ш or щ. Replace it with е.

with Natasha - с Ната́шей

The genitive plural - more endings

Feminine nouns ending in -а lose this letter in the genitive plural:

У Пи́тера мно́го книг.	Peter has a lot of books.
Ско́лько в до́ме ко́мнат?	How many rooms in the house?

Masculine and feminine nouns that end in a soft sign have the ending -ей:

Я была́ там пять дней.	I was there for five days.
У Пи́тера мно́го овоще́й.	Peter has a lot of vegetables.

Masculine nouns ending in -ж, ч, ш or щ also have the ending -ей:

мно́го ключе́й - a lot of keys

Irregular plural forms

цвето́к - "a flower" has the nominative plural цветы́ and genitive plural цвето́в.
стул - "a table" - has the nominative plural сту́лья and genitive plural сту́льев.
друг - "a friend" - has the nominative plural друзья́ and genitive plural друзе́й.

в саду́ - in the garden

Several masculine nouns have the prepositional singular ending -у́ or -ю́. This ending is always stressed:

Пи́тер рабо́тает в саду́.	Peter works / is working in the garden.
Тури́ст в аэропорту́.	The tourist is in the airport.
Живём на да́че, как в раю́!	We live in our dacha, as in Paradise!

With "о" - "about" (Lesson 7), the same nouns use the ending -е:

Пи́тер говори́т о са́де.	Peter is talking about his garden.
Она́ ду́мает об аэропо́рте.	She is thinking about the airport.

The declension of personal pronouns

N	я	ты	он	она́	мы	вы	они́
A	меня́	тебя́	его́*	её*	нас	вас	их*
G	меня́	тебя́	его́*	её*	нас	вас	их*
D	мне	тебе́	ему́*	ей*	нам	вам	им*
I	мной	тобо́й	им*	ей*	на́ми	ва́ми	и́ми*
P	мне	тебе́	нём	ней	нас	вас	них

* After prepositions the forms его́, её, их etc change to него́, неё, них etc.
The prepositional case always uses a preposition.

Мне пора́ идти.	It's time for me to go.
Он о тебе́ говори́т.	He talks about you.
У него́ два туале́та.	He has two toilets.
Он рабо́тает в нём.	He works in it.
Ему́ на́до жени́ться.	He should get married.

Пи́тер игра́ет на гита́ре

With musical instruments the verb игра́ть - "to play" - is used with на and the prepositional case.

Пи́тер игра́ет на гита́ре.	Peter plays the guitar.
Са́ша игра́ет на аккордео́не.	Sasha plays the accordion.

Споко́йной ночи! - Good night!

This is in the genitive case. The verb жела́ть - "to wish", which takes the genitive case, is omitted.

спать - to sleep

я сплю, ты спишь, он / она́ спит, мы спим, вы спи́те, они́ спят

петь - to sing

я пою́, ты поёшь, он / она́ поёт, мы поём, вы поёте, они пою́т

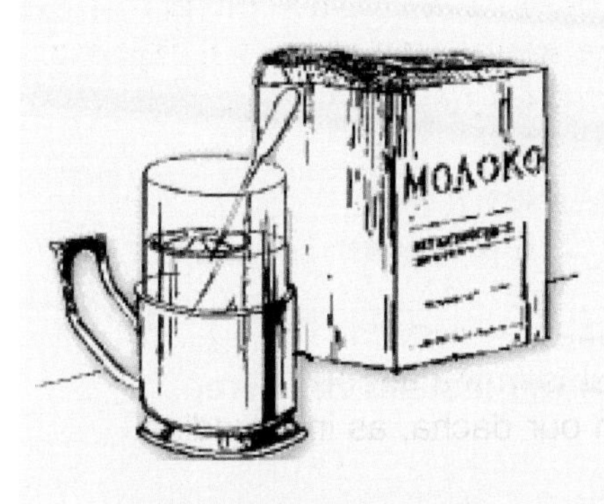

Чай с молоко́м

Чай с лимо́ном

1. Вопро́сы к те́ксту - Questions on the text

а. Людми́ла пьёт чай с лимо́ном или с молоко́м?
б. Где жила́ Людми́ла в Ло́ндоне?
в. Вади́м зна́ет, что Людми́ла жила́ у Пи́тера?
г. Дом Пи́тера - это типи́чный англи́йский дом?
д. У Пи́тера есть балко́н?
е. Како́й телеви́зор у Пи́тера?
ж. Пи́тер живёт оди́н?
з. Что ду́мает Тама́ра о са́де Пи́тера?

2. Peter and Vadim - Complete the dialogue

- А вы живёте в _________ Ло́ндона?
- Нет, но недалеко́ от _________.
- У вас _________?
- Нет, я живу́ в _________.
- Интере́сно. А это _______ дом?
- Нет. Это обы́чный дом. Два __________.
  Но _________ большо́й.
- Очень интере́сно. А ва́ша ______ рабо́тает?
- У меня́ нет ________. Я живу́ с _________.

сад
кварти́ра
до́ме
це́нтре
це́нтра
большо́й
ма́мой
этажа́
жены́
жена́

3. Fill the gaps according to the story and change the ending as necessary

а. Людми́ла пьёт чай с __________.
б. Пи́тер живёт с __________.
в. Тама́ра хо́чет познако́миться с __________.
г. Пи́тер игра́ет в ша́хматы с __________.
д. Ива́н был в теа́тре с __________.
е. Фильм "Из Росси́и с _________".

ма́ть
Пи́тер
молоко́
Людми́ла
Вади́м
любо́вь

4. An exercise to practise case endings. Answer the questions using Пи́тер in your answer

а. О ком вы ду́маете? О Вади́ме? Нет, о Пи́тере!
б. У кого́ есть но́вый биле́т? У Вади́ма? Нет, у _________ !
в. Кто был в гости́нице? Вади́м? Нет, ___________!
г. Кому́ вы звони́те? Вади́му? Нет, ___________!
д. Вы бы́ли в до́ме Вади́ма? Нет, в до́ме __________ !
е. С кем вы игра́ли? С Вади́мом? Нет, с __________!

5. Repeat the same exercise with Людми́ла instead of Пи́тер, and then with other Russian names.

ЧИТАЙТЕ! УРОК 10

You are working for an oil firm in the town of Nefteyugansk in Siberia. The weather is bad and you can't go out. You decide to watch some television. Look at the TV section in the local paper and make a note of programmes which may be of interest. Make a note of the title, time and channel of:

1. Any sports programmes

 ____

 ____

2. Any opportunities to listen to music

 ____

 ____

3. Any programmes of specific relevance to your work in the oil industry

 ____

ТВ ДЛЯ ВАС!

Канал <ОСТАНКИНО>

9.20 Мультфильм
9.25 "Просто Мария"
10.10 Торговый мост
10.40 В мире животных
11.20 Теледоктор
11.50 Волейбол
12.20 Телефильм "Криминальный талант"
13.25 Мультфильм
13.40 Новости
14.30 Теннис
16.10 Блокнот
16.15 Зебра
17.00 Концерт
18.20 Последняя война в Грузии
19.00 "Просто Мария" сериал
19.55 Итоги
20.35 Документальный телефильм
21.50 "Моя вторая мама" - художественный фильм
23.50 Хоккей

Канал <РОССИЯ>

8.55 Концерт
9.15 Панорама новостей
10.10 Нью-Йорк сегодня
11.15 Музыкальный фестиваль в Санкт Петербурге
12.05 "Санта Барбара"
13.10 Российская энциклопедия
13.55 Нефтяные ресурсы Сибири
14.15 Художественный фильм "Я шагаю по Москве"
16.10 Наша железная дорога
17.10 Волшебный мир Диснея
18.25 Кинозвезды говорят
19.00 Военное ревю
19.20 Мультфильм
19.30 "Санта Барбара"
20.00 Что? Где? Когда?
20.45 Дикая природа Америки
21.15 Календарь садовода
21.45 Видеосалон
23.05 Ночное небо

СЛУШАЙТЕ!	**УРОК 10**

96

Tamara is looking for a new flat. Someone telephones:

1. How does the man describe his flat?
2. How big is his kitchen?
3. Where is his flat situated?
4. Tamara jotted down his phone number. Is it correct?

246-89-47

ГОВОРИТЕ!

1. Use the following questions to prepare a short description of your house or flat

- У вас большо́й дом / больша́я кварти́ра?
- У вас два этажа́?
- Каки́е у вас ко́мнаты?
- У вас есть балко́н?
- У вас есть гара́ж?
- У вас есть компью́тер, телеви́зор, телефо́н?
- У вас есть интерне́т?
- Кака́я ме́бель у вас?
- У вас большо́й сад?
- Вы живёте в це́нтре го́рода?

Then compare your house or flat with those of other people in the group.

2. Who are you playing with? - С кем вы игра́ете?
Language game for a group.
Prepare a set of name cards, with first names only.
Ива́н - Бори́с - Ни́на - Ната́ша etc.
Each member of the group picks two or three cards.
These are the people you have to say you are playing with.

In a circle, the first person says who he is playing with:
Пи́тер: Я игра́ю с Ива́ном и с Ни́ной.

The second person repeats this and adds his own statement:
Анна: Пи́тер игра́ет с Ива́ном и с Ни́ной, а я игра́ю с Ка́тей и с Бори́сом.

Carry on round the circle until everyone has had a turn. Help each other if necessary.

Then talk to other people at random, trying to remember who they are playing with.

3. Вы игра́ете на гита́ре?

Find out what instruments people play.

Вы игра́ете на гита́ре? - Нет.
Вы игра́ете на пиани́но? - Нет.
Вы игра́ете на аккордео́не? - Да.
Я то́же игра́ю на аккордео́не - Хорошо́!

You can also talk about what instruments are played by different musicians you know of.

аккордео́н
балала́йка
виолонче́ль
кларне́т
контраба́с
бараба́н
фле́йта
гита́ра
орга́н
пиани́но
роя́ль
саксофо́н
труба́
тромбо́н
скри́пка

www

4. Noun endings practice

Use the name cards you prepared for exercise 2, and some question cards for actions that take different endings, for example the questions in exercise 4 page 122. One person deals out a question card, the next a name card, and you have to give the answer as quickly as possible.

"Я ду́маю о Ната́ше!"

Наташа

О ком вы думаете?

KEY TO THE EXERCISES

УРОК 1 - УПРАЖНЕНИЯ

1. а) ваш. б) моя. в) ваш. г) он. д) она. е) она. ж) он.
2. а) Да, мой. б) Вот она. в) Нет, я бизнесмен. г) Спасибо. д) Нет, это Москва. е) Пожалуйста. ж) Вот он. з) Нет, это аспирин.
3. - Где мой паспорт? - Вот ваш паспорт. - Спасибо. - Пожалуйста

УРОК 1 - ЧИТАЙТЕ!

1. ВЫДАЧА БАГАЖА - Luggage reclaim, ТРАНЗИТ - Transit, № РЕЙСА - Flight number, КРАСНЫЙ КОРИДОР - Red channel, НЕ КУРИТЬ - No Smoking, ПАСПОРТНЫЙ КОНТРОЛЬ - Passport control, РЕГИСТРАЦИЯ - Check in, ТУАЛЕТ - Toilet, СУВЕНИРЫ - Souvenirs, ВЫХОД - Exit, ПАРФЮМЕРИЯ - Perfume shop, ВЫХОДА НЕТ - No exit.
2. Suggested answers: паспорт, икона, наркотик, виски, доллар, декларация.
3. Dollar, Pound, Rouble, Euro, Japanese yen, Chinese yuan, Indian rupee.
4. Ford, Renault, Mercedes, Lada, Fiat, Jaguar, Moskvich, BMW, Volvo, Citroen, Volga, Cadillac, Toyota. - Lada, Moskvich, Volga.
5. Sheremetyevo-2, Domodyedovo.

УРОК 1 - ПИШИТЕ! Richard Branson, Mary Smith, John Phillip Thomas.

УРОК 1 - СЛУШАЙТЕ!

1. Passport, visa, declaration. 2. Tourism. 3. London, Cambridge, Birmingham, Manchester, Windsor, Liverpool. 4. Yes.

УРОК 2 - УПРАЖНЕНИЯ

1. а) метро, б) план, в) Идите, г) сумка, д) понимаете, е) пожалуйста, ж) знаю, з) близко, и) ваш.
2. Кинотеатр - прямо и направо. Театр - прямо и налево. Буфет - прямо и налево. Ресторан - прямо. Метро - прямо и направо.
3. Идите! - Go! / Скажите! - Tell (me)! / Извините! - Excuse (me)! / Слушайте! - Listen! Читайте! - Read! / Идите прямо! - Go straight! / Идите направо! - Go right! Идите налево! - Go left! / Пишите! - Read!

УРОК 2 - ЧИТАЙТЕ И ПИШИТЕ!

1. Birmingham, Edinburgh, Bristol, Manchester, London, Coventry, Liverpool, Oxford.
2. Simpson and Son Ltd., Nicholas Robertson
3. МУЗЕЙ - Museum, МЕТРО - Subway, СТОЯНКА ТАКСИ - Taxi rank, УЛИЦА - Street, ТУРИЗМ - Tourism, ИНТУРИСТ - Intourist, КАССА - Ticket office, КИОСК - Kiosk, МЕДПУНКТ - First Aid Point ПРОСПЕКТ - Avenue, МИЛИЦИЯ - Police, РЕМОНТ - Under repair, ТЕАТР - Theatre, ЦЕНТР - Centre
4. Scrambled towns:

```
    Т О М С К М О С К В А
        У
П Е Т Е Р Б У Р Г
Е       М
Р   В Л А Д И В О С Т О К
М       Н
Ь       С
    И Р К У Т С К
С А Р А Н С К     О М С К
```

УРОК 2 - СЛУШАЙТЕ!

1. Smolenskaya.
2. No.
3. Улица Веснина.

УРОК 3 - УПРАЖНЕНИЯ

1. а) Да. б) Нет. в) Нет. г) Нет. д) Нет. е) Нет. ж) Нет
2. а) Не очень. б) Да. в) Нет. г) Нет. д) Нет.
3. а) Можно. б) понимаю. в) вас. г) знаете. д) визы. е) гостиницы. ж) вас. з) для / мамы.
4. а) Четыре. б) Семь. в) Девять. г) Три. д) Ноль.

УРОК 3 - ЧИТАЙТЕ!

1. 1. Пётр Степанович. 2. Борис Владимирович. 3. Нина Петровна. 4. Иван Николаевич. 5. Галина Борисовна. 6. Марина Павловна.
2. Елена/Егор - Иванова Мария Алексеевна/Нудин

УРОК 3 - СЛУШАЙТЕ!

1. Nephew (Sister's son). 2.Saransk. 3.Nina. 4.No.

УРОК 4 - УПРАЖНЕНИЯ

1. а) Он работал. б) Да, она была в Лондоне. в) Нет, он из Саранска. г) Да, он был в Лондоне. д) Да, он обедал.
2. а) в центре. б)в чемодане. в) в ресторане. г) на поезде.
3. а) были. б) был. в) была. г) был. д) были. е) делали. ж) работали. з) знал/был. и) ждал
4. - Что вы делали в Лондоне?
   - Я работала.
   - А где в Лондоне вы работали?
   - Я работала в центре.
   - А где вы жили?
   - Я жила в гостинице.
5. а) знаю. б) думаете. в) обедаете. г) работает. д) понимают. е) знаешь, работает. ж) обедаем.

УРОК 4 - СЛУШАЙТЕ! 1. No. 2. No. 3.The Hilton.

УРОК 4 - ЧИТАЙТЕ И ПИШИТЕ! Извините. Я забыл/-ла. Я работал/-ла в Лондоне.

УРОК 5 - УПРАЖНЕНИЯ

1. а) Нет б) Да в) Да г) Да д) Нет е) Нет ж) Да з) Нет.
2. а) был б) есть в) открыт г) закрыта д) заказал е) смотрите ж) работает з) смотрит.
3. - Я вас приглашаю в ресторан.
   - Очень хорошо! А когда?
   - Завтра, в час.
   - Хорошо! А где?
   - Здесь в ресторане в гостинице.
4. а) Иван смотрит телевизор. б) Бар закрыт. в) Зоя Петровна в ресторане. г) Касса закрыта. д) Людмила работает в Москве. е) Мы знаем Петербург. ж) Они не понимают.

УРОК 5 - СЛУШАЙТЕ!

1. Mikhail Sergeyevich. 2. Today. 3. On Arbat. 4. Yes. 5. Ivan's phone number (293 2526).

УРОК 6 - УПРАЖНЕНИЯ

1. а) Да. б) Да. в) Да. г) Людмила. д) Иван. е) Чёрный. ж) Белый. з) Не один.
2. - Смотрите, вот Вадим!
   - А что он здесь делает?
   - Я не знаю, что он делает.
   - А он не один!
   - Да, он не один!
   - Какой сюрприз!
   - Приятного аппетита!
3. Что вы хотите?
   Я хочу салат и вино.
   А я хочу икру, хлеб и водку.
   Я хочу икру и бутылку вина.
   Я тоже хочу вино.
   Хорошо! Девушка, принесите, пожалуйста, салат, вино, икру, хлеб и водку.

УРОК 6 - СЛУШАЙТЕ!

1. She is allergic to it. 2. Red wine. 3. Red wine, salad, caviare, salami. 4. Good, but very expensive.

УРОК 7 - УПРАЖНЕНИЯ

1. а) Да. б) Ходить в кино, в театр, смотреть телевизор...в) Нет. г) Нет. д) Нет. е) Да. ж) Нет.
2. а. Иван живёт и работает в Саранске.
   б. Людмила любит смотреть телевизор.
   в. Вадим часто приглашает Людмилу в кино.
   г. Саранск большой индустриальный город.
   д. Людмила идёт домой.
3. - Что вы делаете в свободное время?
   - Я люблю читать книги.
   - А вы любите ходить в кино?
   - Да, конечно люблю.
   - А сегодня вы идёте на оперу?
   - Да, иду.
   - Кто вас приглашает?
   - Миллионер!
4. Стюардесса говорит об аэропорте.
   Актёр говорит о театре.
   Почтальон говорит о почте.
   Программист говорит о компьютере.
   Журналист говорит о журнале.
   Космонавт говорит о космосе.
   Музыкант говорит о музыке.
   Кинокритик говорит о фильме.
   Шофёр говорит о такси.
   Тракторист говорит о тракторе.

УРОК 7 - ЧИТАЙТЕ И ПИШИТЕ!

1. а) Нижний Новгород. б) Санкт-Петербург. в) Иркутск. г) Москва.

УРОК 7 - СЛУШАЙТЕ!

1. In the restaurant of the hotel Mars.
2. That Vera thought that Ivan was Lyudmila's husband. 3. Yes. 4. No.

УРОК 8 - УПРАЖНЕНИЯ

1. а) Да. б) Нет. в) Да. г) Да. д) Да. е) Нет. ж) Нет. з) Да. и) Нет.
2. - Алло
   - Кто говорит?
   - Это Питер. Вы меня помните?
   - Конечно, помню. Какие у вас планы на сегодня?
   - У меня нет планов.
   - Пожалуйста, приезжайте к нам.
   - С удовольствием. А когда?
   - Приезжайте в восемь часов.
   - Очень хорошо!
3. а. Туристы читают журналы.
   б. Туристки читают книги.
   в. Инженеры были здесь.
   г. Новые студенты тоже были здесь.
   д. Магазины открыты.
   е. Это новые телевизоры?
   ж. Английские бизнесмены не говорят по-русски.
4. а. Кинокритик обедает.
   б. Это русский город.
   в. Ресторан открыт.
   г. Это хороший билет.
5. В Москве много автобусов, театров, парков и туристов. В Москве мало каналов.

УРОК 8 - ЧИТАЙТЕ

1. Sergei Esenin, Bulat Okudzhava - Vagankovsky cemetery. The others - Novodyevichy cemetery.
2. Televisions, video recorders, video cameras, music centres, compact disk players, copying machines, calculators, computers, printers, food items, electrical household appliances. From Japan, China, Korea.

УРОК 8 - СЛУШАЙТЕ

1. The Bolshoy theatre. 2. Tomorrow.
3. The opera "Снегурочка" because it was in the evening. 4. At 7 pm.

УРОК 9 - УПРАЖНЕНИЯ

1. а) Нет. б) Нет. в) Да. г) Нет. д) Да. е) Да.
2. - Зоя Петровна? Добрый вечер!
   - Добрый вечер. Вы в театре?
   - Да, я в театре.
   - А как вам нравится опера?
   - Мне очень нравится. Прекрасная опера.
   - А когда она кончается?
   - Она кончается поздно. Не надо меня ждать.
3. Людмила говорит Зое Петровне, что завтра она идёт к врачу, но она говорит Ивану, что она идёт к подруге.
4. Аршавин играет в футбол. Буре́ - хоккей. Каспаров - шахматы. Шарапова - теннис. Шевченко - футбол. Южный - теннис.

УРОК 9 - ЧИТАЙТЕ И ПИШИТЕ

1. Puss in Boots. June 21st at 8 pm.
2. Igor Lagutin - Soldier, Larissa Kornyeva - Princess, Victor Ivanov - Cat.
3. M. Shapiro.

УРОК 9 - ЧИТАЙТЕ

1. а) At the Kremlin Palace. б) Napoleon Bonaparte. в) Presidential Orchestra of the Russian Federation.
2. а) On Sunday September 22nd at 4 pm on Manezhnaya square. б) To dictatorship. в) Yes.

УРОК 9 - СЛУШАЙТЕ

1. After the theatre. 2. Yes. 3. No. 4. No.

УРОК 10 - УПРАЖНЕНИЯ

1. а) С молоком. б) У Питера. в) Нет. г) Да. д) Нет. е) Большой телевизор. ж) Нет. з) Ей не интересно.
2. - А вы живёте в центре Лондона?
   - Нет, но недалеко от центра.
   - У вас квартира?
   - Нет, я живу в доме.
   - Интересно. А это большой дом?
   - Нет. Это обычный дом. Два этажа. Но сад большой.
   - Очень интересно. А с кем вы живёте? С женой?
   - У меня нет жены. Я живу с мамой.
3. а) молоком. б) матерью. в) Питером. г) Вадимом. д) Людмилой. е) любовью.
4. Нет, о Питере! / Нет, о Людмиле!
   Нет, у Питера! / Нет, у Людмилы!
   Нет, Питер! / Нет, Людмила!
   Нет, Питеру! / Нет, Людмиле!
   Нет, в доме Питера! / Нет, в доме Людмилы!
   Нет, с Питером! / Нет, с Людмилой!

УРОК 10 - ЧИТАЙТЕ!

1. 11:50 am - Volleyball. 2:30 pm - Tennis. 11:50 pm - Ice Hockey. All Ostankino.
2. 8:55 am - Concert - Rossiya, 11:15 am - Musical festival in St. Petersburg - Rossiya, 5:00 pm - Concert - Ostankino.
3. Oil resources of Siberia - 1:55 pm - Rossiya.

УРОК 10 - СЛУШАЙТЕ!

1. One room. All facilities. Large. Light. 2. Not very. 3. On Arbat. 4. No. 246-89-74.

LISTENING TEXTS

These are the texts of the listening exercises from each lesson. The dialogues are intended for general comprehension practice. They include some grammar points you will not have met in the lessons, and some new words which you will find in the dictionary.

1. АЭРОПОРТ

16

Тамо́женник: Ваш па́спорт, пожа́луйста.
Людми́ла: Вот..., пожа́луйста.
Тамо́женник: А где ва́ши ви́за и деклара́ция?
Людми́ла: Вот.
Тамо́женник: Так.. хорошо́. Вы прие́хали из Англии?
Людми́ла: Да.
Тамо́женник: С како́й це́лью вы е́здили в Англию?
Людми́ла: Тури́зм.
Тамо́женник: Каки́е города́ вы посети́ли?
Людми́ла: Ло́ндон, коне́чно. Я там жила́. ... Кро́ме э́того: Ке́мбридж, Би́рмингем, Манче́стер, Ви́ндзор, Ливерпу́ль...
Тамо́женник: Что у вас в багаже́?
Людми́ла: Оде́жда, сувени́ры, фотоаппара́т...
Тамо́женник: Вот ваш па́спорт. Проходи́те.

2. УЛИЦА

26

Ива́н: Скажи́те пожа́луйста, что это за зда́ние?
Прохо́жий: Это музе́й Пу́шкина.
Ива́н: А метро́ “Смоле́нская” отсю́да далеко́?
Прохо́жий: Нет, это бли́зко. Де́сять мину́т. А вам куда́?
Ива́н: Мне нужна́ у́лица Веснина́, дом де́сять.
Прохо́жий: Да, это бли́зко от метро́ “Смоле́нская”. Иди́те пря́мо, и у́лица Веснина́ нале́во.
Ива́н: Спаси́бо.
Прохо́жий: Не́ за что.

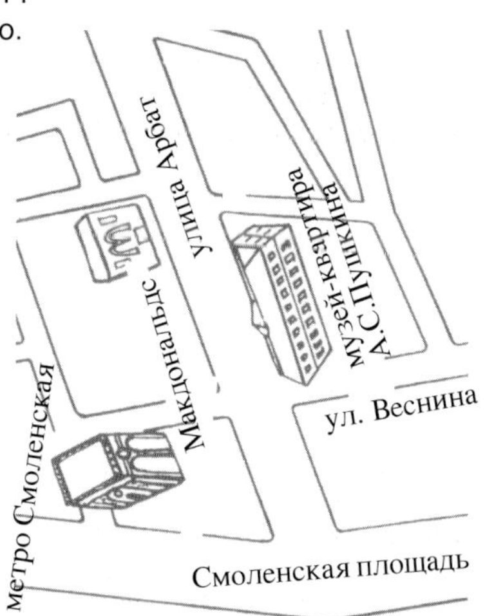

32 **3. СЕМЬЯ**

Людми́ла:	Зо́я Петро́вна, а кто э́тот Ива́н?
З. Петро́вна:	Ива́н? Мой племя́нник. Сын мое́й сестры́. Я то́же из Сара́нска. У меня́ в Сара́нске сестра́. А Ива́н её сын.
Людми́ла:	Пра́вда? Вы из Сара́нска?! А как зову́т ва́шу сестру́?
З. Петро́вна:	Её зову́т Ни́на... Ни́на Петро́вна. Я её о́чень давно́ не ви́дела.
Людми́ла:	Так Иван и Вади́м не знако́мы?
З. Петро́вна:	Да, не знако́мы.
Людми́ла:	Как интере́сно!

38 **4. ГДЕ ВЫ БЫЛИ?**

Людми́ла:	Вади́м, как ты ду́маешь, Ива́н бога́тый?
Вади́м:	Ду́маю, миллионе́р.
Людми́ла:	Почему́ ты так ду́маешь?
Вади́м:	Я, коне́чно, не зна́ю..., но... Сара́нск большо́й го́род... А как ты ду́маешь, что он де́лал в Ло́ндоне? Сара́нск... Ло́ндон... бизнесме́н... да! Ду́маю, он миллионе́р!
Людми́ла:	А ты то́же миллионе́р?
Вади́м:	Ну что ты, Лю́дочка! Ты же меня́ зна́ешь. Я не миллионе́р. Ты лу́чше скажи́ мне, где ты жила́ в Ло́ндоне?
Людми́ла:	Я жила́ ... в гости́нице... в гости́нице Хи́лтон.
Вади́м:	Это далеко́ от це́нтра?
Людми́ла:	Это в са́мом це́нтре. Недалеко́ от Гайд Па́рка.

51 **5. ГОСТИНИЦА**

М.С.:	Алло́!
Ива́н:	Михаи́л Серге́евич? Здра́вствуйте! Это Ива́н Козло́в говори́т.
М.С.:	Козло́в из Сара́нска? Вы уже́ в Москве́? Когда́ прилете́ли?
Ива́н:	Сего́дня.
М.С.:	Где вы останови́лись?
Ива́н:	В гости́нице "Марс". Зна́ете э́ту гости́ницу? Она́ на Арба́те.
М.С.:	Ну, прекра́сно! Это недалеко́. Так мы вас ждём за́втра. У вас а́дрес есть?
Ива́н:	Да, а́дрес есть.
М.С.:	Ну прекра́сно! А како́й у вас там телефо́н?
Ива́н:	Телефо́н? Сейча́с. Запиши́те. 293 2526.
М.С.:	Хорошо́! 293 2526. Записа́л. До за́втра.
Ива́н:	До за́втра.

59 **6. РЕСТОРАН**

Вади́м:	Ве́ра, что вы хоти́те на заку́ску?
Ве́ра:	А что у них есть?
Вади́м:	Хоти́те икру́?
Ве́ра:	Нет, спаси́бо. Икру́ мне нельзя́. У меня́ от икры́ аллерги́я.
Вади́м:	А пить что вы хоти́те?
Ве́ра:	Если мо́жно, кра́сное вино́.
Вади́м:	Ну, коне́чно, мо́жно. ... Де́вушка, принеси́те, пожа́луйста буты́лку кра́сного вина́, сала́т, икру́ и колбасу́. Пока́ всё, а там - посмо́трим.
Ве́ра:	А здесь о́чень непло́хо!
Вади́м:	Да, рестора́н о́чень хоро́ший, но, к сожале́нию, о́чень дорого́й.

7. О СЕБЕ

69

Ве́ра:	Вади́м, кто э́то сиде́л в рестора́не в гости́нице "Марс"?
Вади́м:	А... э́то моя́ о́чень хоро́шая знако́мая... Её зову́т Людми́ла.
Ве́ра:	Людми́ла... А э́то был её муж?
Вади́м:	Её муж?! Ха-ха-ха... нет! Это не её муж. Это мой провинциа́льный ро́дственник - бизнесме́н, миллионе́р из Сара́нска.
Ве́ра:	Миллионе́р? Вы серьёзно? Это о́чень интере́сно! Расскажи́те о нём.
Вади́м:	Со́бственно говоря́, я его́ совсе́м не зна́ю. Мы познако́мились вчера́.
Ве́ра:	Ну, тогда́ познако́мьте меня́ с ним.
Вади́м:	Посмо́трим...

8. ВРЕМЯ

77

Ива́н:	Алло́! Это театра́льная ка́сса?
Де́вушка:	Да, что вы хоти́те?
Ива́н:	Мо́жно заказа́ть биле́ты в Большо́й теа́тр?
Де́вушка:	Когда́ вы хоти́те пойти́?
Ива́н:	У вас есть биле́ты на за́втра?
Де́вушка:	На за́втра? Сейчас посмотрю́. Да, есть два биле́та на бале́т Чайко́вского "Щелку́нчик". Нача́ло в два часа́ дня. Вам о́чень повезло́!
Ива́н:	В два часа́ дня? Нет, э́то не подхо́дит. А на ве́чер есть биле́ты?
Де́вушка:	Ве́чером идёт о́пера "Снегу́рочка".
Ива́н:	А биле́ты есть?
Де́вушка:	Биле́тов мно́го.
Ива́н:	Когда́ начина́ется спекта́кль?
Де́вушка:	В семь часо́в.
Ива́н:	Отли́чно. Мне на́до два биле́та. Моя́ фами́лия Козло́в.
Де́вушка:	Хорошо́.

9. ТЕАТР

89

Тама́ра:	Так ты из теа́тра, так по́здно?! Уже оди́ннадцать часо́в!
Людми́ла:	Да. Извини́, что я так по́здно.
Тама́ра:	Это твой миллионе́р тебя́ пригласи́л в теа́тр? Как его́ зову́т?
Людми́ла:	Ива́н...
Тама́ра:	Ах, да! Ива́н Козло́в, ты мне говори́ла. И что вы смотре́ли?
Людми́ла:	"Снегу́рочку".
Тама́ра:	Я забы́ла, это бале́т и́ли о́пера?
Людми́ла:	Опера, коне́чно. Ты "Снегу́рочку" не смотре́ла?
Тама́ра:	Не смотре́ла. Но меня́ интересу́ет твой миллионе́р. Когда́ мо́жно с ним встре́титься?
Людми́ла:	Тама́ра, я не зна́ю. Он о́чень за́нят.

10. ДОМ

96

Тама́ра:	Алло́!
Мужчи́на:	Я звоню́ по по́воду кварти́ры.
Тама́ра:	Да. Я вас слу́шаю.
Мужчи́на:	У меня́ однoко́мнатная кварти́ра со все́ми удо́бствами.
Тама́ра:	Опиши́те кварти́ру.
Мужчи́на:	Больша́я све́тлая ко́мната, большо́й балко́н и ку́хня.
Тама́ра:	Ку́хня больша́я?
Мужчи́на:	Не о́чень.
Тама́ра:	Поня́тно... А где нахо́дится кварти́ра?
Мужчи́на:	В са́мом це́нтре. На Арба́те.
Тама́ра:	На Арба́те? Это интере́сно!
Мужчи́на:	Да. Это о́чень удо́бное ме́сто.
Тама́ра:	Хорошо́. Я поду́маю и позвоню́ вам. Да́йте мне ваш телефо́н.
Мужчи́на:	Меня́ зову́т Васи́лий Никола́евич. Мой телефо́н: 246-89-74.

GRAMMAR REFERENCE

This is a summary of the grammatical points that you meet in Ruslan 1. Further grammatical points will be introduced in Ruslan 2 and Ruslan 3.

Nouns - Gender
Russian nouns have three genders: masculine, feminine and neuter. You can normally tell the gender by the noun ending. See pages 21, 35 and 99.

Cases
Russian has six cases. Nouns and pronouns decline according to number and case. Adjectives decline according to number, gender and case.

The nominative case is used for the subject of a sentence or for naming an object.

The accusative is used for the direct object, after в and на meaning "to", in certain expressions of time, and after спаси́бо за.

The genitive is used to express "of" and after a large number of prepositions, including у, из, от, для, о́коло, без and напро́тив. It is used after expressions of quantity such as мно́го and after нет to express "none of". The genitive singular of nouns is used after numbers 2, 3, 4, 22, 23, 24, 32, 33, 34, etc. and the genitive plural is used after numbers 5-20, 25-30, 35-40, etc. Certain verbs also take the genitive case.

The dative is used for indirect objects and after к - "towards" - and по - "along".

The instrumental is used with с to express "with".

The prepositional is used after в and на meaning "at" or "in", or after о - "about".

More uses of the cases are given in Ruslan 2 and Ruslan 3.

In Ruslan1 you have met all the regular singular case endings of nouns, and some of the plural endings.

Masculine noun endings

	hard	**-ь**	**-ж, -ч, -ш, -щ**	**-ай**	
N	биле́т	гость	ключ	трамва́й	SINGULAR
A	биле́т	го́стя*	ключ	трамва́й	
G	биле́та	го́стя	ключа́	трамва́я	
D	биле́ту	го́стю	ключу́	трамва́ю	
I	биле́том	го́стем	ключо́м	трамва́ем	
P	биле́те	го́сте	ключе́	трамва́е	
N	биле́ты	го́сти	ключи́	трамва́и	PLURAL
A	биле́ты	госте́й*	ключи́	трамва́и	
G	биле́тов	госте́й	ключе́й	трамва́ев	
D	биле́там	гостя́м	ключа́м	трамва́ям	
I	биле́тами	гостя́ми	ключа́ми	трамва́ями	
P	биле́тах	гостя́х	ключа́х	трамва́ях	

*the accusative of animate masculine nouns is the same as the genitive.

Neuter noun endings

	-о	-е	-ие	-мя	
N	ме́сто	мо́ре	зда́ние	вре́мя	SINGULAR
A	ме́сто	мо́ре	зда́ние	вре́мя	
G	ме́ста	мо́ря	зда́ния	вре́мени	
D	ме́сту	мо́рю	зда́нию	вре́мени	
I	ме́стом	мо́рем	зда́нием	вре́менем	
P	ме́сте	мо́ре	зда́нии	вре́мени	
N	места́	моря́	зда́ния	времена́	PLURAL
A	места́	моря́	зда́ния	времена́	
G	мест	море́й	зда́ний	времён	
D	места́м	моря́м	зда́ниям	времена́м	
I	места́ми	моря́ми	зда́ниями	времена́ми	
P	места́х	моря́х	зда́ниях	времена́х	

Feminine noun endings

	-а	-га, -ка, etc.	-я	-ия	-ь
N	ви́за	кни́га	неде́ля	деклара́ция	пло́щадь
A	ви́зу	кни́гу	неде́лю	деклара́цию	пло́щадь
G	ви́зы	кни́ги	неде́ли	деклара́ции	пло́щади
D	ви́зе	кни́ге	неде́ле	деклара́ции	пло́щади
I	ви́зой	кни́гой	неде́лей	деклара́цией	пло́щадью
P	ви́зе	кни́ге	неде́ле	деклара́ции	пло́щади
N	ви́зы	де́вушки	неде́ли	деклара́ции	пло́щади
A	ви́зы	де́вушек*	неде́ли	деклара́ции	пло́щади
G	виз	де́вушек	неде́ль	деклара́ций	площаде́й
D	ви́зам	де́вушкам	неде́лям	деклара́циям	площадя́м
I	ви́зами	де́вушками	неде́лями	деклара́циями	площадя́ми
P	ви́зах	де́вушках	неде́лях	деклара́циях	площадя́х

*the accusative plural of animate feminine nouns is the same as the genitive.

Spelling rules

When endings change, certain consonants force a soft vowel.
1. ы cannot follow г, к, ж, х, ч, ш or щ. It is replaced by и.
The genitive singular of кни́га is therefore кни́ги.
2. unstressed о cannot follow ж, ц, ч, ш or щ. It is replaced by е.
The feminine instrumental "with Natasha" is therefore с Ната́шей.

Exceptions

Some masculine nouns have prepositional sing. in -у́ or -ю́. в саду́ - "in the garden".
Some masculine nouns have a nominative plural in -а́. города́ - "towns".
цвето́к - "a flower" has the nominative plural цветы́ and genitive plural цвето́в.
стул - "a table" - has the nominative plural сту́лья and genitive plural сту́льев.
друг - "a friend" - has the nominative plural друзья́ and genitive plural друзе́й.
мать and дочь have a stem in -ер-. с ма́терью - "with mother".
Many nouns have a "fleeting" о or е. день - "a day". два дня - "two days".
There are often changes of stress. See the declension of ме́сто and гость.

There are more unusual declensions and exceptions, which you will meet in Ruslan 2 and Ruslan 3.

Personal pronouns

N	я	ты	он	она́	мы	вы	они́
A	меня́	тебя́	его́	её	нас	вас	их
G	меня́	тебя́	его́	её	нас	вас	их
D	мне	тебе́	ему́	ей	нам	вам	им
I	мной	тобо́й	им	ей	на́ми	ва́ми	и́ми
P	мне	тебе́	нём	ней	нас	вас	них

After prepositions, его́, её, ему́, их, etc. change to него́, неё, нему́, них:

He has. У него́ есть.
with her - с ней
about them - о них

The question words кто - "who" and что - "what"

N	кто	что	D	кому́	чему́
A	кого́	что	I	кем	чем
G	кого́	чего́	P	ком	чём

Adjectives

You have so far only met nominative endings. See pages 75 and 99.

Possessive pronouns

You have met the nominative forms мой / моя́ / моё / мои́ and ваш / ва́ша / ва́ше / ва́ши твой - "your" (familiar and singular) and наш - "our" change in the same way.

Russian verbs in the present

First conjugation ending in -ать

знать - я зна́ю, ты зна́ешь, он / она́ / оно́ зна́ет, мы зна́ем, вы зна́ете, они́ зна́ют
понима́ть - я понима́ю, ты понима́ешь, он / она́ понима́ет, ...
рабо́тать - я рабо́таю, ты рабо́таешь, он / она́ рабо́тает, ...
ду́мать - я ду́маю, ты ду́маешь, он / она́ ду́мает, ...
обе́дать - я обе́даю, ты обе́даешь, он / она́ обе́дает, ...
спра́шивать - я спра́шиваю, ты спра́шиваешь, он / она́ спра́шивает, ...
чита́ть - я чита́ю, ты чита́ешь, он / она́ чита́ет, ...
де́лать - я де́лаю, ты де́лаешь, он / она́ де́лает, ...
приглаша́ть - я приглаша́ю, ты приглаша́ешь, он / она́ приглаша́ет, ...

Other first conjugation verbs

жить - я живу́, ты живёшь, он / она́ / оно́ живёт, мы живём, вы живёте, они́ живу́т
ждать - я жду, ты ждёшь, он / она́ ждёт, мы ждём, вы ждёте, они́ ждут

Second conjugation verbs

говори́ть - я говорю́, ты говори́шь, он / она́ / оно́ говори́т, мы говори́м, вы говори́те, они́ говоря́т
смотре́ть - я смотрю́, ты смо́тришь, он/она́ смо́трит, мы смо́трим, вы смо́трите, они́ смо́трят

Second conjugation verbs with consonant changes in the first person

люби́ть - я люблю́, ты лю́бишь, он / она́ / оно́ лю́бит, мы лю́бим, вы лю́бите, они́ лю́бят
ходи́ть - я хожу́, ты хо́дишь, он / она́ хо́дит, мы хо́дим, вы хо́дите, они́ хо́дят

Irregular verbs

хоте́ть - я хочу́, ты хо́чешь, он / она́ / оно́ хо́чет, мы хоти́м, вы хоти́те, они́ хотя́т
мочь - я могу́, ты мо́жешь, он / она́ мо́жет, мы мо́жем, вы мо́жете, они́ мо́гут

Russian verbs in the past

There are four endings:

masculine -л feminine -ла neuter -ло plural -ли

Here are some typical conjugations:

знать - я знал / зна́ла, ты знал / зна́ла, он знал, она́ зна́ла, оно́ зна́ло
мы / вы / они́ зна́ли

ждать - я ждал / ждала́, ты ждал / ждала́, он ждал, она́ ждала́, оно́ ждало́,
мы/вы/они́ жда́ли

быть - я был / была́, ты был / была́, он был, она́ была́, оно́ бы́ло,
мы /вы / они́ бы́ли

The perfective aspect

You have met some verbs in the perfective aspect:

заказа́ть - to book
забы́ть - to forget.

So far you have met these verbs either in the infinitive or in the past tense:

Мо́жно заказа́ть но́мер? Is it possible to book a room?
Вы забы́ли? Did you forget?

Don't try to change these verbs to form a present tense. This would in fact give you a perfective future tense instead. Verb aspects and future tenses are in Ruslan 2.

Imperative verb forms

Here are some imperative forms that you meet in Ruslan 1.
The polite or plural form вы is given:

Иди́те!	-	Go!	Дава́йте!	-	Lets ...!
Откро́йте!	-	Open!	Проходи́те!	-	Come through!
Извини́те!	-	Excuse (me)!	Скажи́те!	-	Tell (me)!
Чита́йте!	-	Read!	Слу́шайте!	-	Listen!
Найди́те!	-	Find!	Принеси́те!	-	Bring (me) ... !

To form the singular familiar form remove the -те ending:

Иди́!	-	Go!	Дава́й!	-	Lets ...!
Откро́й!	-	Open!	Проходи́!	-	Come through!

etc.

Иди́те пря́мо!

RUSSIAN - ENGLISH DICTIONARY

This section contains the vocabulary in this book, and additional vocabulary used in the Ruslan 1 multimedia CD-ROM, workbook and reader. Where words have more than one meaning, the meaning(s) used in this course have been given.

а	and, but
авиакомпа́ния	airline
Австра́лия	Australia
австрали́ец / -и́йка	an Australian
автопортре́т	self-portrait
администра́тор	administrator
аккордео́н	accordion
актёр	actor
аллерги́я	allergy
Алло́!	Hello! (on the phone)
Аме́рика	America
америка́нец / -ка	an American
америка́нский	American (adj.)
анана́с	pineapple
англича́нин / -ка	Englishman / woman
англи́йский	English (adj.)
Англия	England
анекдо́т	anecdote / joke
анке́та	questionnaire
антра́кт	interval (theatre)
апельси́н	an orange
аперити́в	aperitif
апре́ль	April
ара́бский	Arabian (adj.)
аргуме́нт	argument (reason)
арифме́тика	arithmetic
а́рмия	army
арти́ст	artist (performing)
аспири́н	aspirin
афга́нский	Afghan (adj.)
аэропо́рт	airport
ба́бушка	grandmother
бага́ж	baggage
бадминто́н	badminton
балала́йка	balalaika
бале́т	ballet
балко́н	balcony
Ба́лтика	the Baltic
бана́н	banana
банк	bank (money)
банкома́т	cash machine
бар	bar
бараба́н	drum
баскетбо́л	basketball
бе́гать	to run
бейсбо́л	baseball
бе́лый	white
Бе́льгия	Belgium
бельэта́ж	dress circle
беспла́тный	free (of charge)
бефстро́ганов	beef Stroganoff
бе́рег	bank (river etc.)
беспла́тный	free (of charge)
би́знес	business
бизнесме́н	businessman / -person
биле́т	ticket
благодари́ть	to thank
бланк	form
бли́зко	near
блин	pancake
блу́зка	blouse
блю́до	dish, course (of a meal)
бога́тый	rich
большо́й	big
больни́ца	hospital
борщ	beetroot soup
ботани́ческий	botanical
брази́льский	Brazilian
брат	brother
брита́нский	British
бу́ква	letter (character)
бу́ду, бу́дет etc.	will be
буты́лка	bottle
буфе́т	snack bar
бы́вший	former
быть	to be
бюдже́т	budget
бюро́	bureau, office
в (+ acc.)	to / into
в (+ prep.)	at / in
валли́ец / валли́йка	Welshman / -woman
вальс	waltz
валю́та	hard currency
вам	for you / to you
Варша́ва	Warsaw
варе́нье	jam
вас	you (object)
вас зову́т	your name is
ваш / ва́ша etc.	your
вдруг	suddenly
вегетариа́нец / -ка	vegetarian
везде́	everywhere
велосипе́д	bicycle
вера́нда	veranda
ве́чер	evening
вещь (f.)	thing, item
вид	type / view
видеока́мера	video camera
ви́деть	to see
ви́за	visa
визи́тка	visiting card
вино́	wine
виолонче́ль (f.)	cello
вку́сный	tasty

вме́сте	together
внизу́	downstairs
внима́ние	attention
внук	grandson
вну́чка	granddaughter
вода́	water
во́дка	vodka
возвра́тный	reflexive
возвраща́ться	to return
вокза́л	station (main)
Во́лга	Volga River
волейбо́л	volleyball
вопро́с	question
воро́та	gates
восемна́дцать	eighteen
во́семь	eight
во́семьдесят	eighty
воскресе́нье	Sunday
вот	here is / there is
Вот как!	Oh, really!
врач	doctor
вре́мя	time
все	everybody / all
всегда́	always
всё	everything / all
всё в поря́дке	everything is OK
вста́вить (perf.)	to insert
встре́титься (perf.)	to meet
встре́ча	meeting
вто́рник	Tuesday
второ́й	second
вчера́	yesterday
вы	you (polite or plural)
вы́брать (perf.)	to choose
вы́дача багажа́	luggage reclaim
вы́ставка	exhibition
вы́ход	exit (pedestrian)
выходно́й	day off
газ	gas
газе́та	newspaper
гармо́нь (m.)	harmonica
где	where (at)
генера́тор	generator
Герма́ния	Germany
гита́ра	guitar
гитари́ст	guitarist
гла́вный	main
глаго́л	verb
говори́ть	to say / to speak
год	year
голла́ндский	Dutch
Голла́ндия	Holland
гольф	golf
гора́	hill, mountain
го́род	town
горя́чий	hot (of food)
гости́ная	living room
гости́ница	hotel
гость (m.)	guest

госуда́рственный	state (adj.)
граждани́н / -а́нка	citizen
гражда́нство	nationality
грамм	gram
Гре́ция	Greece
гре́ческий	Greek (adj.)
грузи́н / -ка	a Georgian
грузи́нский	Georgian (adj.)
Гру́зия	Georgia
да	yes
Дава́й(те) ...	Let's ...
давно́	for a long time
да́же	even
Да́йте ...!	Give ... !
далеко́	far
Да́ния	Denmark
дартс	darts
да́та	date
да́тельный	dative
дать	to give
да́ча	dacha, summer house
два	two
два́дцать	twenty
двена́дцать	twelve
де́вушка	young lady
девяно́сто	ninety
девятна́дцать	nineteen
Дед Моро́з	Father Frost
де́душка / дед	grandfather
дежу́рный / -ая	person on duty / attendant
действи́тельно	really
дека́брь	December
деклара́ция	declaration
де́лать	to do
де́ло	business
день	day
день рожде́ния	birthday
де́ньги	money
дере́вня	village / countryside
деревя́нный	wooden
десе́рт	dessert
де́сять	ten
де́ти	children
де́тский сад	kindergarten
диало́г	dialogue
дива́н	sofa, couch
диктату́ра	dictatorship
дирижёр	conductor (music)
для (+ gen.)	for
до (+ gen.)	until / as far as / up to
До свида́ния!	Good bye!
До́брое у́тро!	Good morning!
До́брый ве́чер!	Good evening!
дово́льно	rather, quite
докуме́нт	document
до́ктор	doctor (form of address)
до́лго	for a long time
до́ллар	dollar

дом	house / block of flats
дорого́й	dear / expensive
достиже́ние	achievement
дочь	daughter
друг	friend
друго́й	another
друзья́	friends
ду́мать	to think
душ	shower
дя́дя	uncle
Евро́па	Europe
е́вро	euro / euros
Египе́т	Egypt
его́	him
его́	his
еди́нство	unity
её	her (possessive)
её	her (object)
е́здить	to go (regularly, transport)
ей	to her, for her
ему́	to him, for him
е́сли	if
е́хать	to go (transport)
ещё	again / else
ёлка	New Year tree
Как жаль!	What a pity!
жа́реный	roasted
ждать	to wait
же	then (adds emphasis)
жена́	wife
железнодоро́жный	railroad (adj.)
жени́ться	to get married (man)
же́нский	women's
жето́н	a token
жить	to live
журна́л	journal
журнали́ст (-ка)	journalist
забы́ть (perf.)	to forget
заводи́ть (imp.)	to start (something)
за́втра	tomorrow
за́втрак	breakfast
зада́ть вопро́с (perf.)	to ask a question
заказа́ть (perf.)	to book
зака́зывать (imp.)	to book
зако́нчить (perf.)	to complete
закры́т	closed
заку́ска	starter (food)
зал	hall (large room)
заливно́й	in aspic
заме́тка	note
вы́йти за́муж	to get married (woman)
за́нят / -а́ / -о / -ы	busy
за́падный	western
записа́ть (perf.)	to write down
запо́лнить (perf.)	to fill in
защи́тник	protector
звони́ть	to call, to phone
зда́ние	building
здесь	here
Здра́вствуйте!	Hello!
зе́бра	zebra
земля́	earth
знако́м	acquainted
знако́мий / -ая	acquaintance
зна́чит	that means
Зо́лушка	Cinderella
зоопа́рк	zoo
и	and
и т.д.	etc.
игра́ть	to play
иде́я	idea
Иди́те!	Go! / Come!
идти́	to go (on foot)
ие́на	yen
из (+ gen.)	from
изве́стный	well-known
Извини́те!	Excuse (me)!
ико́на	icon
икра́	caviare
и́ли	or
императи́в	imperative
и́мя	first name
индустриа́льный	industrial
инициати́ва	initiative
инжене́р	engineer
иностра́нец / -ка	foreigner
инструме́нт	instrument
интере́сно	it is interesting
интере́сный	interesting
интерне́т	Internet
инти́мный	intimate
инфинити́в	infinitive
инфля́ция	inflation
информа́ция	information
Ирла́ндия	Ireland
ирла́ндец / -ка	Irishman / woman
ирла́ндский	Irish (adj.)
Испа́ния	Spain
испа́нский	Spanish (adj.)
Ита́лия	Italy
италья́нский	Italian (adj.)
их	their
ию́ль	July
ию́нь	June
к (+ dat.)	towards
к нам	to our place
к сожале́нию	unfortunately
кабине́т	office
ка́ждый	every, each
ка́жется	it seems
как	how
Как дела́?	How are things?
как-то раз	once (upon a time)
како́й	what kind of / which
калькуля́тор	calculator
ками́н	fireplace
Кана́да	Canada
кана́дец / -ка	a Canadian

кана́дский	Canadian (adj.)
кана́л	canal
ка́рта	card / map
карти́на	picture
ка́рточка	card
карто́фель (m.)	potato (the plant)
карто́шка	potato (the food)
каска́д	cascade
ка́сса	cash desk
кассе́та	cassette
кафе́	cafe
квалифика́ция	qualification
кварти́ра	flat
квас	drink made from rye bread or black bread
кероси́новый	paraffin (adj.)
кефи́р	thin yoghurt
килогра́мм	kilogram
кинломе́тр	kilometre
кино́	the cinema
кинокри́тик	cinema critic
кинотеа́тр	a cinema
кио́ск	kiosk
Кита́й	China
кита́йский	Chinese (adj.)
кла́дбище	cemetery
кло́ун	clown
кларне́т	clarinet
класси́ческий	classical
клие́нт	client
клуб	club
ключ	key
кни́га	book
кни́жный	book (adj.)
ковёр	carpet
когда́	when
колбаса́	salami
колле́га	colleague
коло́дец	a well
командиро́вка	business trip
комите́т	committee
коммента́рий	commentary
ко́мната	room
компа́кт-диск	compact disk
компью́тер	computer
коне́чно	of course
консульта́нт	consultant
контраба́с	double bass
контро́ль (m.)	control; check; test
конча́ться	to finish
коня́к	cognac
Коре́я	Korea
коридо́р	corridor
коро́ль (m.)	king
космона́вт	cosmonaut
ко́смос	space
костёр	campfire
кот	cat
котле́та	meatball
Кото́рый час?	What's the time?
котте́дж	detached house
ко́фе (m.)	coffee
краси́вый	beautiful
кра́сный	red
креди́тный	credit (adj.)
кремль (m.)	kremlin, fortress
кре́пость (f.)	fortress
кре́сло	armchair
кре́йсер	cruiser
кри́зис	crisis
крите́рий	criterion
ксе́рокс	xerox
кто	who
Ку́ба	Cuba
куда́	where (to)
культу́рный	cultured / cultural
купи́ть (perf.)	to buy
кури́ть	to smoke
курс	course
ку́хнн	kitchen; cuisine
ла́дно	fine, all right
ла́мпа	lamp
ле́вый	left
легко́	it is easy
лес	forest
ле́то	summer
лимо́н	lemon
лимона́д	lemonade
лимо́нный	lemon (adj.)
лови́ть	to catch
ло́жа	box (theatre)
луна́	moon
лу́чше	better
лы́жи	skis
люби́ть	to love
любо́вь (f.)	love
мавзоле́й	mausoleum
магази́н	store, shop
май	May
ма́ло	little, not much
маргари́н	margarine
март	March
ма́сло	oil; butter
мать	mother
ме́бель (f.)	furniture
медбра́т	male nurse
медве́дь (m.)	bear
медпу́нкт	first aid point
медсестра́	nurse (f.)
междунаро́дный	international
мемора́ндум	memorandum, memo
ме́неджер	manager
меню́	menu
меня́	me
меня́ зову́т	my name is
ме́тод	method
ме́сто	seat / place
ме́сяц	month

метро́	metro, underground
мечта́	dream (daydream)
мили́ция	police
миллионе́р	millionaire
минера́льный	mineral
Мину́точку!	Just a minute!
ми́нус	minus
ми́тинг	demonstration, rally
мне	for me / to me
мно́го	a lot, many
мно́жественный	plural
моби́льник	mobile phone
моде́ль (f.)	model (of a car etc.)
мо́жет быть	perhaps
мо́жно	it is possible
мой, моя́, etc.	my
молоде́ц	good boy / girl
Молоде́ц!	Well done!
молодо́й	young
молоко́	milk
монасты́рь	monastery
моро́з	frost
моро́женое	ice cream
моско́вский	Moscow (adj.)
мост	bridge
мотоци́кл	motorcycle
мочь	to be able to
муж	husband
мужчи́на	man
музе́й	museum
му́зыка	music
музыка́льный	musical
музыка́нт	musician
мы	we
на (+ acc.)	to / onto
на (+ prep.)	at / on
на по́езде	by train, rail
на са́мом де́ле	in fact
на у́лице	outside
наве́рно	probably
наверху́	upstairs
на́до	it is necessary
Не на́до!	Don't!
на́дпись (f.)	sign
нажа́ть (perf.)	to click, to press
наза́д	(go) back
найти́ (perf.)	to find
назва́ние	name (of towns, etc.)
наконе́ц	at last
нале́во	to the left
напи́сано	written
напи́ток	a drink
напра́во	to the right
наприме́р	for example
напро́тив (+ gen.)	opposite
нарко́тик	drug / drugs (narcotic)
наро́д	people
наро́дный	people's
настоя́щий	present (time) / real
натура́льный	natural
находи́ться	to be located
национа́льный	national
нача́ло	beginning
начина́ться	to begin
наш, на́ша, etc.	our
не	not
Не на́до!	Don't!
недалеко́	not far
неде́ля	week
незави́симость	independence
нельзя́	not allowed, must not
не́мец / -ка	a German
неме́цкий	German (adj.)
немно́жко	a little bit
нет	no
нефть (f.)	crude oil
ничего́	nothing / all right
но	but
новозела́ндец /-ка	New Zealander
Новозела́ндия	New Zealand
но́вый	new
ноль (m.)	zero
но́мер	hotel room / number
ноя́брь	November
нра́виться	to please
ну!	well! (exclamation)
ну́жен	needed
о (+ prep.)	about
о себе́	about oneself
обе́д	dinner / main meal
обе́дать	to have dinner
обме́н	exchange
объе́кт	object
обы́чный	usual
о́вощи	vegetables
овся́нка	oatmeal porridge
огоро́д	vegetable garden
оде́жда	clothing
оди́н	one / alone
оди́ннадцать	eleven
однoко́мнатный	one-room (adj.)
о́зеро	lake
окно́	window
окро́шка	clear soup (cold, with kvas)
октя́брь	October
он	he / it
она́	she / it
оно́	it
о́пера	opera
опла́та	payment
опла́чивать	to pay for
оптими́ст	optimist
орга́н	organ (instrument)
организа́ция	organisation
осетри́на	sturgeon
остановиться	to stay
от (+ gen.)	from
отве́т	reply, answer

отдыха́ть	to rest
оте́ц	father
оте́чество	fatherland
откры́т	open
отли́чный	excellent
отправле́ние	departure
отсю́да	from here
о́тчество	patronymic name
о́фис	office
официа́нт / -ка	waiter / waitress
о́чень	very
парк	park
парте́р	stalls (theatre)
партнёр	partner
парфюме́рия	perfume shop
па́спорт	passport
па́спортный	passport (adj.)
пассажи́р	passenger
пельме́ни	small stuffed dumplings
пе́рвый	first
перево́д	translation
перево́зка	transportation
переры́в	break (from work etc.)
перестро́йка	perestroika
переу́лок	side street
перехо́д	pedestrian crossing (above or below ground)
пери́од	period
пешко́м	on foot
печь (f.)	stove
пиани́но	upright piano
пи́во	beer
пиро́г	pie
пи́сьменный	writing (adj.)
письмо́	letter (correspondance)
пла́вать	to swim
план	plan / map
плане́та	planet
племя́нник	nephew
племя́нница	niece
пло́хо	it is bad
плохо́й	bad
пло́щадь (f.)	square
плюс	plus
по (+ dat.)	along
по-англи́йски	in English
по-ру́сски	in Russian
по де́лу	on business
по по́воду (+ gen.)	in connection with
побе́да	victory
повезло́	was lucky
пода́рок	a present
подва́л	cellar
по́дпись (f.)	signature
подру́га	girlfriend
по́езд	train
пожа́луйста	please / you're welcome
по́здно	late
Пойдёмте!	Let's go! (on foot)
пока́	while / for now
Пока́!	So long!
покупа́ть	to buy
поликли́ника	polyclinic
полити́ческий	political
по́лка	shelf
по́льский	Polish (adj.)
По́льша	Poland
помидо́р	tomato
по́мнить	to remember
по́мощь (f.)	help
понеде́льник	Monday
понима́ть	to understand
пора́	it's time
Португа́лия	Portugal
портфе́ль (m.)	briefcase
поря́док	order
по́сле (+ gen.)	after
посмотре́ть (perf.)	to have a look
постро́ить (perf.)	to build
посыла́ть	to send
пото́м	then
потому́ что	because
похоро́нен	is buried
почему́	why
по́чта	post, post office
почтальо́н	postman
почти́	almost
почто́вый и́ндекс	post code
по́яс	belt / zone
прав	right (short adj.)
пра́вда	the truth
пра́вда?	isn't it? / right?
Пра́вда	Pravda (the newspaper)
пра́вильный	correct (adj.)
пра́здник	holiday
пра́ктика	practice
предложе́ние	sentence (gram.) / proposal
Президе́нт	President
прекра́сный	wonderful
прибы́тие	arrival
приве́т	a greeting
Приве́т!	Hi!
приглаша́ть	to invite
прие́зд	arrival (by transport)
Приезжа́йте!	Come! (by transport)
прие́хать (perf.)	to arrive (by transport)
прилага́тельное	adjective
прилёт	arriving flight, arrival
Принеси́те!	Bring!
принима́ть	to accept
принoси́ть	to bring
при́нтер	printer
прихо́жая	entrance hall
прия́тный	nice, pleasant
пробле́ма	problem
провинциа́льный	provincial
програ́мма	programme

программи́ст	programmer
програ́ммка	programme (theatre)
продолже́ние	continuation
проду́кты	food products
прое́кт	project
про́пуск	a pass
проси́ть	to ask (a favour)
прослу́шать (perf.)	to listen
проспе́кт	avenue
Прости́те!	I'm sorry!
профессиона́льный	professional
профе́ссия	occupation
профе́ссор	professor
прочита́ть (perf.)	to read
Проходи́те!	Come through!
прохо́жий / -ая	passer-by
проце́нт	percent
проше́дший	past (adj.)
пря́мо	straight ahead
пье́са	a play (theatre)
пятна́дцать	fifteen
пя́тница	Friday
пять	five
пятьдеся́т	fifty
рабо́та	work
рабо́тать	to work
рад	glad
ра́дио	radio
раз	time, occasion
рай	Paradise
ра́но	early
ра́ньше	before
рассказа́ть (perf.)	to tell
револю́ция	revolution
регистра́ция	registration / check-in
рейс	flight
река́	river
ремо́нт	repairs
репортёр	reporter
рестора́н	restaurant
речно́й	river (adj.)
Рим	Rome
ро́дственник / -ца	relative
рожде́ние	birth
Рождество́	Christmas
роль (f.)	role
романти́чный	romantic
Росси́я	Russia
росси́йский	Russian
роя́ль (m.)	grand piano
рубль (m.)	rouble
рупи́я	rupee
ру́сский	Russian
ры́ба	fish
ры́нок	market
рюкза́к	rucksack
ряд	a row
ря́дом	nearby
с (+ gen.)	from
с (+ instr.)	with
сад	garden
Сади́тесь!	Sit down!
саксофо́н	saxophone
сала́т	salad; lettuce
самова́р	samovar
самолёт	a plane
самопрове́рка	self test
са́нки	sled
сапоги́	boots
сара́й	shed
све́тлый	light (adj.) (color)
свобо́дный	free (having freedom / vacant)
свой	one's own / my own etc.
свято́й	holy
свято́й	a saint
себя́	oneself
сего́дня (sivodnya)	today
сего́дня ве́чером	this evening
сейф	a safe
секре́т	a secret
секрета́рь (m.)	secretary
секре́тный	secret (adj.)
селёдка	herring
семина́р	seminar
семна́дцать	seventeen
семь	seven
се́мьдесят	seventy
семья́	family
сентя́брь	September
сертифика́т	certificate
сестра́	sister
сиби́рский	Siberian
Сиби́рь (f.)	Siberia
систе́ма	system
Скажите!	Tell!
сказа́ть	to say
ско́лько?	how much?
скоре́е	more quickly
Скоре́е!	Hurry up!
скри́пка	violin
сла́дкий	sweet (adj.)
сле́ва	on the left
сле́довать	to follow
слова́рь (m.)	dictionary
сло́во	word
слу́шать	to listen
слы́шать	to hear
слы́шно	audible
смотре́ть	to look at
снача́ла	to start with
снег	snow
Снегу́рочка	the Snowmaiden
собира́ться	to gather together
собо́р	cathedral
сове́тский	Soviet
совсе́м	quite
содержа́ние	content
сок	juice

соли́ст	soloist
солове́й	nightingale
соля́нка	soup from pickled or salted vegetables
со́рок	forty
со́товый телефо́н	mobile phone
со́ус	sauce
спа́льня	bedroom
спаси́бо	thank you
спать	to sleep
спекта́кль (m.)	show
специали́ст	specialist
Споко́йной но́чи!	Good night!
спо́нсор	sponsor
спорт	sport
спра́ва	on the right
спра́шивать	to ask
среда́	Wednesday
стадио́н	stadium
ста́нция	station (small)
ста́рый	old
ста́тус	status
стена́	wall
стихотворе́ние	poem
сто	one hundred
сто́ить	to cost
стол	table
сто́лик	small table
столи́ца	capital city
столо́вая	dining room
стоя́нка такси́	taxi rank
страна́	country
страни́ца	page
студе́нт	student
студе́нтка	female student
стул	chair
сту́лья	chairs
стюарде́сса	stewardess
суббо́та	Saturday
сувени́р	souvenir
су́мка	handbag
суп	soup
существи́тельное	noun
счёт	bill
США	USA
сын	son
сыр	cheese
сюрпри́з	surprise
табло́	display board
так	so / in this way
та́кже	also
такси́	taxi
такси́ст	taxi driver
таксофо́н	public phone
там	there (at)
тамо́жня	customs
тамо́женник	customs officer
育 тарака́н	cockroach
твой, твоя́ etc.	your (familiar)
теа́тр	theatre
текст	text
телеба́шня	television tower
телеви́зор	TV set
телегра́ф	telegraph office
те́лекс	telex
телефо́н	telephone
те́ннис	tennis
термина́л	terminal
терминоло́гия	terminology
тепе́рь	now
тётя	aunt
типи́чный	typical
тогда́	then, in that case
то́же	also
то́лько	only
тома́тный	tomato (adj.)
традицио́нный	traditional
трактори́ст	tractor driver
трамва́й	tram
транзи́т	transit
три	three
три́дцать	thirty
трина́дцать	thirteen
три́ста	three hundred
тро́йка	three-horse sleigh
тролле́йбус	trolleybus
тромбо́н	trombone
труба́	trumpet / pipe
труд	labour
туале́т	toilet
туда́	there (to)
тури́зм	tourism
тури́ст / -ка	tourist
ты	you (familiar)
у вас	you have / at your home
у меня́	I have / at my home
удо́бный	comfortable / convenient
удо́бство	convenience / facility
удово́льствие	pleasure
узна́ть (perf.)	to find out
уже́	already
у́жин	supper
у́жинать	to have supper
Украи́на	Ukraine
украи́нец / -ка	a Ukrainian
украи́нский	Ukrainian (adj.)
у́лица	street
на у́лице	in the street; outdoors
улыба́ться	to smile
универса́льный	universal
университе́т	university
упражне́ние	exercise
уста́л	tired
у́тро	morning
у́тром	in the morning
учи́тель	teacher
учи́тельница	female teacher
Уэ́льс	Wales

факс	fax
факт	fact
фами́лия	family name, last name
февра́ль	February
федера́ция	federation
фи́рма	firm
флаг	flag
фле́йта	flute
фойе́	foyer
фотоаппара́т	camera
фотогра́фия	photograph
Фра́нция	France
францу́зский	French
фрукт	a fruit
фрукто́вый	fruit (adj.)
фунт	pound
футбо́л	football
футболи́ст	football player
хлеб	bread
ходи́ть	to go (regularly, by foot)
хозя́йство	economy
хокке́й	ice hockey
холоди́льник	fridge
холо́дный	cold (adj.)
хор	choir
хоро́ший	good
хорошо́	it is good / OK
хоте́ть	to want
храм	temple
худо́жественный	art (adj.)
царь	tsar
цветно́й	colour(-ed) (adj.)
цвето́к	a flower
цель (f.)	purpose
цеме́нт	cement
центр	centre
центра́льный	central
цирк	circus
цифр	numeral
цыплёнок	young chicken
чай	tea
час	an hour / one o'clock
часово́й по́яс	time zone
ча́сто	often
часы́ (pl.)	clock, watch
челове́к	person
чемода́н	suitcase
чемпио́н	champion
черда́к	attic
чёрный	black
четве́рг	Thursday
четы́ре	four
четы́рнадцать	fourteen
число́	date / number
чита́ть	to read
чте́ние	reading
что	what / that
Что тако́е ...?	What is ...?
шампа́нское	champagne
ша́пка	fur hat
ша́хматы	chess
шашлы́к	shish kebab
Швейца́рия	Switzerland
шестна́дцать	sixteen
шесть	six
шестьдеся́т	sixty
шко́ла	school
шокола́д	chocolate
шотла́ндец /-ка	Scotsman / -woman
Шотла́ндия	Scotland
шофёр	driver
шту́ка	piece
Щелку́нчик	Nutcracker
щи	cabbage soup
эконо́мика	economy
экономи́ст	economist
экспе́рт	expert
экспре́сс	express
электри́чество	electricity
электро́нная по́чта	email
эскала́тор	escalator
эта́ж	floor (e.g. first floor)
э́тот, э́та, etc.	this
эффе́кт	effect
юа́нь	yuan (Chinese currency)
ю́мор	humour
юри́ст	lawyer
я	I
я́блоко	apple
я́года	berry
янва́рь	January
Япо́ния	Japan
япо́нский	Japanese (adj.)
я́рус	circle (in the theatre)

Ру́сский алфави́т

а б в г д е ё ж з и й
к л м н о п р с т у ф
х ц ч ш щ ъ ы ь э ю я